YIANNIS DESYPRIS

ARGOSARONIC islands

AEGINA - POROS - HYDRA - SPETSES
ANGISTRI - SALAMINA

EDITIONS
TOUBI'S®
ΕΚΔΟΣΕΙΣ

ATHENS 2002

Text: Yiannis Desypris
Photographs:Michalis Toubis S.A. Archives, Y. Desypris
Artistic Editor: Evi Damiri
Editor: Daphne Christou
Translation: Despina Christodoulou

Colour separation, printing: M. TOUBIS GRAPHIC ARTS S.A.

Copyright © 2002 M. TOUBIS EDITIONS S.A.   Nisiza Karela, Koropi, P.O. Box 194 00
                                                 Tel. 010-6029974, 010-6645548 Fax: 010-6646856
                                                 INTERNET: http://www.toubis.gr

ISBN: 960-540-442-7

CONTENTS

CONTENTS

HYDRA

SPETSES

The port of Dapia, Spetses.

The islands of the Argolic and Saronic Gulfs are priceless jewels, gracing both gulfs with their bountiful beauty. The Athenians are lucky that they can reach these islands in such a short time, far from the noisy city. The closest, historic Salamis, is also the most populated. From Perama in Attica it takes only ten minutes to cross over to Paloukia opposite, and from there you can go wherever you want around the island in a car. Further south, beautiful Aegina with its pine trees, sandy beaches and the famous Temple of Aphaia is only an hour by boat from Piraeus. Aegina also has a large population, but not as large as Salamis. Next to it is the small, green island of Angistri.

Further to the south is pretty Poros, opposite the Peloponnese, and even further is the famous Hydra, as well-known as Mykonos, with its traditional architecture. At the entrance of the Argolic Gulf is Spetses, picturesque and green. With a long nautical tradition, its fleet and brilliant sailors played an important role in the Greek War of Independence against the Turks.

The furthest island, luscious-green Spetses, is three hours by boat from Piraeus. If the journey were to be undertaken by hydrofoil, which services all these islands (except Salamis), then the journey time would be reduced to about a third. The islands of the Saronic and Argolic Gulfs provide an opportunity for both a brief escape to paradise from Athens, as well as - why not? - a long holiday. The name of these Gulfs is more often than not shortened to Argosaronic.

OSARONIC

A brief escape to paradise

Hydra, woodcut by Grammatopoulos, 90 x 120 cm., 1980.

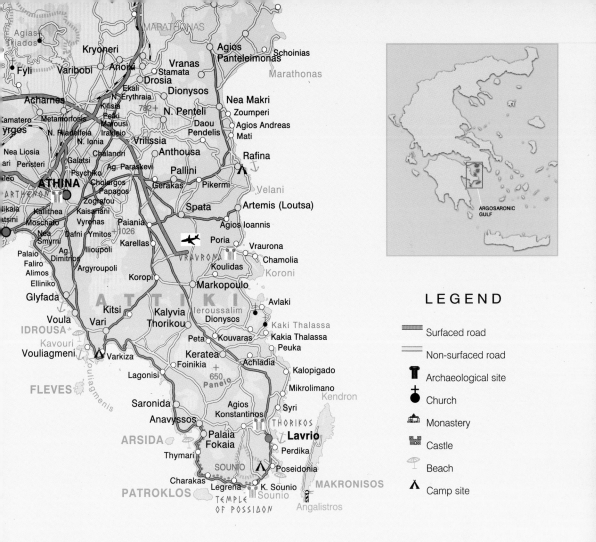

Three of the five largest islands of the Argosaronic - Salamis, Aegina and Poros - are located within the Saronic Gulf, the gulf between the coasts of Attica and the Peloponnese. There is a rich ancient Greek mythology relating to these islands, and the mythology of the gulf that surrounds them is just as abundant. It is said that it took its name from Saron, the King of ancient Troezen in the Peloponnese, opposite Poros. Once when hunting a deer, Saron fell into the sea and drowned. From then on the gulf was named the Saronic.

In addition to ancient Troezen, this part of the Peloponnese has other interesting features. The Methana peninsula is here, with its dormant volcano and therapeutic springs. Not to mention the pretty little ports of Palia and Nea Epidaurus and, especially, the ancient theatre of Epidaurus, where ancient tragedies are staged in the summer.

Hydra, along with the island of Dokos which is today uninhabited, is situated between the Saronic and the Argolic Gulfs. Spetses, as we mentioned, lies at the entrance of the Argolic Gulf, a gulf which belongs exclusively to the Peloponnese, at the edge of which is Nafplion, one of the most beautiful towns of Greece. The Argolic Gulf took its name from the historic city of Argos, which is near Nafplion.

One can visit the most interesting wider area of the Argosaronic from these islands in the summer.

SALAMIS

Whenever one thinks of Salamis, his or her thoughts automatically go back 2,500 years. To then when the famous naval battle between the Greeks and the Persians took place between its straits. The Greeks won and the enemy from Asia withdrew completely. Historians have wondered as to what the fate of western civilisation would have been if the Greeks had lost this battle.

Today there are almost no traces on the island to testify to what happened here in 480 BC. There are simply the same straits in which the naval battle took place, the beautiful island, the magnificent Argosaronic, the pine-covered mountains, the pretty gulfs and their coves. Only that now the majority of these gulfs and coves have been filled with densely-populated summer resorts. I say most of them, because there are still secluded beaches and isolated fish

To the echo of history

tavernas on the southern coast. Of course, the island's capital, old Koulouri, could not have remained an exception to this growth, and has developed and evolved into a modern town with its port and its large fishing fleet. The other resorts have also grown. There is now a good road network and bus routes which connect all the resorts. This road network extends to the more sparsely populated areas, giving the visitor the opportunity to enjoy the beautiful forests and indented coastlines of the island, and even to visit its two important monasteries: Faneromeni and Ayios Nikolaos (St Nicholas). One can reach the island from Perama, which is opposite Piraeus, and the journey by ferry boat takes only ten minutes to Paloukia in Salamis. A visit to Salamis can be a pleasant day trip, an overnight stop or - and why not? - a much longer stay at one of its pretty beaches. A stay most certainly with many surprises and experiences in store.

Aianteio

SALAMINA

N

Batsi

Limanaki

MT.MBATSI

VASILIKA BAY

Vasilika

Ano
Vasilika

M.Kim. Theotokou
Faneromenis

Vromopoysi

Psili
Amos

PALIAMBELA

142

Steno

Agios
Georgios

136

MT. SAMARI

AGIOS

GEORGIOS

IS. MAKRONOSOS

Iliakti

Xeno

MT. LOUKEZES

SALAMINA

IS. REVITHOUSA

MT. RESTI

260

Galini

Agios
Ioannis

CAPE KARAS

Vathi

Resti

Agia
Paraskeuv

SALAMINA BAY

269

CAPE
PETRITIS

375

MT. KOKKINOS VRAHOS

MT.MAUROV

THERIO

M. Ipapandis

Aianteio

Zarmbala

MT. VIGL
366

MT. MEGA STEFANI

MT. KARELA

KAKI
VIGLA

239

347

Agios
Haralambos

M. Agiou
Nektariou

MT. PROF. ILIAS

235

IS. KANAKIA

M. Agiou
Nikolaou

340

KANAKIA

Karakiani

MT. NTARNIZA

Perani

Dimitra

Gialia

194

PERANI BAY

CAPE
KANAKIA

PYRGIGONI

Agios
Georgios

GKINANI

IS. PERA

LAMPRINO

Agios
Dimitrios

Eas Club

LAMPRINO

MT. KOHI

276

Peristeria

CAPE MERTZANI

Kolones

IS. PERISTERIA

CAPE KOGHI

Geography

Salamis, nested away in the inlet of the Saronic Gulf, with only two narrow straits dividing it and the earth of Attica. The strait to the east of the island is 1,200 metres wide and the one to the west is only 500 metres wide. This tight embrace with the Attic mainland forms the closed gulf of Elevsina to the north of the island. Salamis, the largest island of the Argosaronic, has an area of 95 square kilometres, a coastline of 104 km., and a population of almost 30,000. The majority of the inhabitants live in the capital, the coastal town of Salamis - also known as Koulouri - whilst the remainder are scattered around the various villages. The coasts of Salamis have many gulfs and pretty capes, and settlements - mainly summer resorts - have grown up within them. Most of the traffic from Attica passes through the port of Paloukia.

Morphology

Covered in pine trees, especially in the south, Salamis has two valleys which divide its mountain area into three sections. The first valley lies between Koulouri and Paloukia and the second between Aianteio (Moulki) and Kaki Vigla. Mavrovouni (367 m.), the island's highest mountain, is in the centre of the island, whilst there is a stream in the south running alongside the Monastery of Ayios Nikolaos. It has two sources and discharges into the bay of Kanakia; it is believed to be the ancient river Vokaro.

CAPE PETRA ALOGIROU

+ 212
ATHMOS

CAPE ARAPIS

+ 147

IS. AGIO GEORGIOS

Kamatero

AMPELAKIA BAY

CAPE KINOSOULA

ANCIENT PORT SALAMINA
+119

Kinosoura

SELINIA BAY

CAPE TROPEA

abia

CAPE TOURLA

KAKI VIGLA BAY

ERANI

LEGEND

Surfaced road
Non-surfaced road
Archaeological site
Church
Monastery
Castle
Beach
Camp site

SALAMINA

MYTHOLOGY & HISTORY

1

The close relationship between Ajax and Achilles is a central feature of the island's mythology.
The photograph shows a black-figure vase by the painter Exekias, depicting the two heroes playing dice
(Rome, Vatican Museum, ca 530 BC).

Mythology

Mythology tells us that the island took its name from the nymph Salamis, daughter of the river god Asopos. Zeus fell in love with Salamis and brought her to the island. Here she gave birth to their child Kycheras, who became the island's first king. Telamon, son of the legendary king of Aegina Aiakos, had fled to the island of Salamis after the murder of his brother Fokos. Kycheras had no sons, but he gave his daughter Glauke in marriage to Telamon, also handing over his throne to him.

Glauke died without leaving any children behind her and Telamon then married Eriboea, with whom he had Ajax (Aias), the patron hero of Salamis. Ajax was leader of the Salaminians and the Megarians during the Trojan War. It was he who took the body of the dead Achilles to the Greek camp, risking his own life.

It had been said at the time that Achilles' armour would be given to the person who had contributed the most to the war effort, and it was eventually given to Odysseus. Ajax considered this to be a great injustice and he became so downhearted that he killed himself. His heroism inspired the greatest tragic poets; indeed, one of Sophocles' seven surviving plays is named after him. We also know that the ancient Greeks honoured Ajax with the Ajaxian Games. For archaeologists the discovery of the remains of his palace is a challenge equal to that of finding the remains of Odysseus' palace on Ithaki.

History

The first inhabitants of Salamis arrived in the neolithic period. This can be seen from the finds in the south of the island. There are also finds from the Mycenean period, during which the island flourished. The prehistoric city was built at Kolones, on the island's southern coast, and was moved in the historic period to the site between today's Kamatero and Ambelakia. This was the ancient city known as Kolouri, a name which, with a slight variation to Koulouri, the inhabitants still use for their capital as well as the whole of the island, although the official name for both is Salamis.

Its strategic position made Salamis an object of contention between the Athenians and the neighbouring Megarians, a struggle which the Athenians, led by Solon, eventually won.

The greatest naval battle of antiquity took place in the island's strait in 480 BC. The Persians had defeated Leonidas and his 300 men at Thermopyles and had gone down to Attica in order to bring the war to a final close and make themselves rulers of Greece. The only obstacle in their path was the mighty fleet of the Athenians and their allies, which had to be defeated. The Persian king Xerxes had taken steps to guarantee that this was achieved. He had come himself as the head of, it is said, 1,200 ships which bore 300,000 men. The Athenians could only marshal up less than 400 ships, which were smaller than those of the Persians, and a crew of 85,000 men.

The Athenian general was Themistokles, who had always believed in a leading role for the fleet in the defence of Athens. Themistokles, in a clever ploy, managed to trick the large Persian fleet into engaging in a clash not on the open sea but in the straits of Salamis, where what mattered most was

2

3

1. *"The departure stele."*
   Tomb stone relief from Salamis.
   Piraeus, Archaeological Museum, 330 BC.
2. *Tomb stones of two young hoplite soldiers from Salamis*
   who fell in the Peloponnesian War.
   Piraeus, Archaeological Museum, 420 BC.

not the size and number of the enemy ships but the agility and speed of the Greek ships and the great knowledge that the Greeks had of the straits.

The battle started at dawn, and by the afternoon of the same day the Persians had been vanquished. The ruins of their ships could be seen in the waters whilst the corpses of their dead were floating along the shore. Xerxes, who could not believe his eyes, abandoned the watchtower that had been set up at Aigaleo, the hill lying opposite in Attica, and departed for his distant homeland with the surviving quarter of the boats from his once multitudinous fleet. Greece had escaped the danger, and the whole of Europe along with it.

The subsequent history of Salamis does not differ much from that of the other Argosaronic islands. The island was a refuge for civilians and fighters during the 1821 War of Independence against the Turks. Georgios Karaiskakis, the great hero of the War of Independence, had his headquarters on the island and was also buried here, in accordance with his wishes.

1. The War Memorial and bust of Karaiskakis in Salamis town.
2. Painting of a view of the island of Salamis.

YESTERDAY & TODAY

The visitor to the densely-populated island of Salamis today will find it difficult to believe how much the place has changed in just a few decades. The old people talk of what was once a quiet island with indented coastlines and a few fishing harbours. About the capital Koulouri, with its old houses and flower-filled gardens. The island was indeed like this, but a century ago not a few decades ago. Now, everything has changed. The indented coastlines have become filled with summer resorts and Koulouri has become a modern town. What has not changed is the love of the Salaminians for the sea, something which has its roots in the mists of time, when the island sent its ships to the Trojan War and when the historic naval battle took place in its straits. The centuries have passed since then. Bounded on all sides by Athens,

Megara and Aegina, the powerful cities of the time, Salamis did not have many opportunities to develop and it was only in the 19th century that, thanks to the industriousness, bravery and persistence of the Salaminians, the island created a worthy fleet of its own. So much so, that shipping and commerce flourished in the 20th century. Today the island has one of the largest fishing fleets of Greece, with trawlers and other fishing boats, and fishing along with the naval professions and farming are the island's main occupations.

The older people even remember the local customs, which, with the passing of the years, have either faded away or disappeared completely. The customs relating to the wedding, the supreme social event, are revived every now and then. They do not include the engagement, which was often arranged when the partners were still children, nor match-making. But the basic points of the ritual are still observed. The display of the bride's dowry, the 'making of the bed' during which all the friends place their gifts on the bridal bed, and, of course, the evening meal after the wedding.

In the old days the bride would wear the traditional bridal gown at the wedding, which was far more luxurious than all the other types of dress. The traditional dress of Salamis became the prototype for all the Argosaronic islands. This dress included: the white lace shirt, the 'zipouni' (a waist-length jacket) with gold-embroidered sleeves, the dark red apron with gold embroidery, the impressive skirt, gold-inlaid shoes, a gold necklace and a head scarf.

This is the costume that the young women wore to dance the celebrated traditional dance of the 'trata.'

The local customs may have faded on the island, but this is not the case with the festivals organised when the churches celebrate their feast days, such as that on 15 August, the feast day of the Panayia, at the Monastery of the Faneromeni, which is the largest on the island. The name Faneromeni means 'revealed,' as it was here that an icon of the Panayia, the Virgin Mary, was found.

THE TOWN OF SALAMIS

The town of Salamis, or Koulouri, as the people of the island's capital call it, is only 2 1/2 kilometres from Paloukia, there were the ferryboats moor. The travellers who come from Perama in Attica need only ten minutes to reach the island. Most of those who travel with their cars do not even get out of them, and as soon as they reach Paloukia follow the coastal road to the left. The road to the right leads to the naval dockyards. It all happens so quickly that one does not have enough time to enjoy the surroundings. All that one remembers is the settlement of Kamatero with the large white church on the hill to the left of the gulf and the little islet of Ayios Georgios to the right, the old quarantine with the abandoned houses , the rocky hill above Palouki and the swarm of ferryboats moored at the port, lined up next to each other, waiting their turn to travel on their regular but brief journeys.

The visitors follow, then, the coastal road to the left. Those who are travelling to Koulouri should pass by the first crossing to the left, the one which goes to Ambelakia and Selinia as well as the next crossing which goes towards Moulki. They will then soon come to the coastal road for Koulouri. This wide coastal avenue, with the new houses to the right, gives the image of a new town, one which has little in connection with old Koulouri, with its pretty, old houses and their gardens and flowers.

The fish market on the left at the beginning of the town, with the swarm of fishing boats in front of it, their nets spread out, reminds you that you are on an island with a naval tradition and that many of its inhabitants worked in the merchant navy or are employed in fishing. After the fish market, a large square in front of the sea has an elegant marble war memorial at its centre. A little further down is a marble bust of Georgios Karaiskakis, one of the leaders of the 1821 War of Independence, whose name is closely connected with the island. Both are set on a raised marble stand. Some tall palm trees opposite the war memorial, in front of the town houses, give a touch of grandeur to the area. Behind the town rises the precipitous and rocky hill of Profitis Ilias with a church of the same name perched at its peak. This very tall hill is visible from all around.

The coastal road continues and splits for a while at the splendid church of Ayios Nikolaos. The Archaeological Museum has been stationed temporarily next to it. The seaside tavernas and cafes begin a little further down. The port is more picturesque here. These tavernas and cafes are raised and provide a wonderful view over the sea, which is filled with little boats and caiques. The coast with the rocks or the flower beds give a different picture from the one we have seen up until now. The high point are the keels around the edge of the port.

Fanermomeni Avenue begins opposite the fish market. It goes uphill at first, and crosses through the town. There are two interesting churches with old wall paintings at the upward slope to the left, not far from the beginning of the Avenue. The first is the Panayia Bosko, on a little lane next to the Avenue and a little above the large church of Ayios Minas, with the white and brown stone, its tall belfry and fine wall-paintings.

The local 'Euripides' Conservation and Cultural Centre has offered much to Salamis through its activities. The Library, with its rich holdings, and the

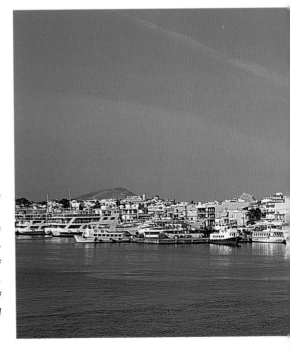

Folk Museum, in which there are exhibits of local traditional dress, paintings, and objects from the war of 1821, are examples of its work.

An open-air theatre has been built on the hill above the town. Various events take place here, such as the Panhellenic Poetry Contest in memory of the great poet Angelos Sikelianos. The view from the theatre of the town's restored windmills and the closed gulf which surrounds it is wonderful.

1. The church of Ayios Minas.
2. Ayios Nikolaos and the Archaeological Museum.
3. Panoramic view from Paloukia.

TOUR OF THE ISLAND

Monastery of the Faneromeni
North Coasts

1. The Ble Limanaki.
2. The Cathedral church of the Monastery of the Faneromeni.

Faneromeni Avenue reaches as far as the western edge of Salamis town and continues until the crossing with Ayios Georgios (St George). The road to the right leads to the north coast, where there is a crossing. Those going to the Monastery of the Faneromeni should take the road to the left. The road to the right leads to Psili Ammos. The whole of this route goes through a pine forest reaching as far as the sea. The Monastery finally appears after you have travelled a total of six kilometres. It looks long. Its tall and white walls have a row of windows on the first floor, yet there are no windows on the ground floor. It has red tiled roofs from which the domes of the cathedral church rise.

This old monastery was most likely founded in the 13th century, and was refounded much later by the Megarian Lambros Kanellos who, as the tradition goes, saw in his sleep the Panayia inviting him to go to the monastery. Kanellos obeyed the Panayia's invitation, went to the island and found her miracle-working icon, which revealed ('fanerothike') itself in front of him. This is why the icon was called the Faneromeni, as was the new monastery which was built again from scratch. Nothing remains of the original monastery, aside from its beautiful cathedral church, a five-domed basilica with many beautiful wall-paintings dating from 1735, amongst which stands out the representation of the Last Judgement.

The Monastery played an important role during the 1821 War of Independence, and successfully withstood many Turkish attacks. During the Second World War it came under threat of disappearance, and so became a nunnery. It was thus saved and able to flourish, so much so that it founded a retirement home for women. Its vestry holds priceless relics. The great poet Angelos Sikelianos lived for many years in a two-storey house belonging to the Monastery, which stands half-ruined at a little distance from it. A bust of the poet stands a few metres away.

The road from the Monastery continues in a westerly direction to Perama. Perama serves as the island's second entry point, this time for travellers coming from the region of Megara. Ferry boat connections from here, however, are less frequent than those from Paloukia. As mentioned above, the road to the east of the Monastery of the Fanermomeni, at the crossing a little before it, leads to the right to Psili Ammos. Here we shall find the little Byzantine church of Ayios Georgios, which resembles that of Ayios Ioannis (St John) Kalyvitis near the Monastery of Ayios Nikolaos Lemonion, which we shall see below. The road continues to Vasilika and the exceptionally charming Ble Limanaki (Little Blue Port), which is built around both sides of the small bay. It terminates at the luscious-green village of Batsi, the houses of which clamber up the slope of the hill, which cuts sharply into the sea.

Kamatero - Ambelakia - Selinia

The first village that the traveller will see on the island as he or she approaches on the boat from Paloukia is Kamatero. Built on a low hill to the left, the brilliant-white church of the Panayia rises grandly high on the peak. Behind the church stretches the archaeological site of the ancient city of Koulouri. Among the remains are the ruins of a tower from the city wall (4th century BC), protected by cordoning and roofing. At another point are the ruins of the Temple.

Ambelakia, 3 km. from Kamatero, has evolved into a modern small provincial town, with more new houses than old. Clean and looked-after, they are built on the site of the ancient city of Koulouri. Indicative of this is the cordoned-off archaeological area in the square of the Tragic Poets in the centre of the town, near to the central square

with the war memorial.

The port of the ancient city was located in the bay of Ambelakia. From there, a long and narrow peninsula, Kynosoura (oura kynos = dog tail) continues to the east and offers a wonderful view towards Perama on the coast of Attica opposite. Between Kynosoura and Perama is a section of the historical strait in which the celebrated Battle of Salamis between the Greek and Persian fleets took place in 480 BC. The hill of Aigaleo can be seen above Perama.

Xerxes, the King of the Persians, had set up his silver throne at its edge so as to follow the course of the battle, during which his large fleet was destroyed. In his tragedy 'The Persians' Aeschylus, the great Greek tragic playwright, has a Persian herald relate to Xerxes' mother the details of the battle:

"And then was heard from the side of the Greeks the cry: Forward the brave children of the Greeks! Now you are fighting for everything!"

The Greeks were indeed fighting for everything at Salamis. For their homeland, their temples and, although they may not have realised it, for all of Europe. Themistokles had the victory trophy set up at Kynosoura, although not a trace of it has survived today.

To the south of Ambelakia is Selinia (6 km.), a delightful coastal resort with well-tended roads, a small pier for the boats which come direct from Piraeus, especially in the summer, and the wonderful church of Ayios Nikolaos with its blue dome in front of the pier. A new asphalt-surfaced road leads from Selinia to Kaki Vigla.

1, 3. Kamatero and the church of the Panayia.
2. The beach at Koulouri.
4 Ayios Nikolaos at Selinia.

Kaki Vigla - Peristeria - Kolones

There are two routes which one can follow to go from Koulouri to Kaki Vigla. One passes through Selinia and is the continuation of the previous route, and the other, which we shall see further below, passes through Moulki. Both these two routes are approximately 11 km. long.

Kaki Vigla is an old inland village in the south of Salamis, and is now a transport node. Its coastal settlement is at a distance of only 1.5 km. and is located at the cove of a gulf which is encircled by a rocky mountain to the left and a pine-covered mountain to the right. In the middle of the gulf there is a beautiful sandy beach, which alternates with a pebbly one, whilst the settlement also spreads out along the slope of the mountain to the left.

From Kaki Vigla and beyond, all the south coast of the island is full of small, pretty bays in which resorts have developed. They are easy to visit as they are almost all connected by an asphalt-surfaced road. Some can even be reached by bus.

Following, then, this asphalt-serviced road, and by-passing Yiala, which can be reached by the dirt road to the left, one can visit Kyriza and neighbouring Perani. From here, one can stop for a little while further up to enjoy the view from high above the Ajax Club. This is a name which has stuck from the days when there was nothing here except for the full (at the time) camp site known as the Ajax Club. Now, villas have been built all around the bay, with gardens which look on high over the sea. Even the rocky little peninsula, which protects the gulf from the wind and the waves, has been built upon. Yet, even now that it is full of houses, the bay is still enchanting.

After the Ajax Club the road passes the village of Halioti, after a while reaching Peristeria, with the islet of the same name opposite. This area, however strange it might seem, has not changed at all, and no new houses have been added here. There are still two fish tavernas here, just as in the old days, and of course the church of Ayios Nikolaos next to the sea, with several little boats and small fishing caiques moored on the rocks in front of the sea.

Above Peristeria is the cave of Euripides. In this cave, which has ten chambers, objects dating to all periods of antiquity have been found. From the neolithic to the Mycenean, to the classical and Roman, and to the period of Frankish rule. A skyphos (cup) with the name of Euripides has also been found. This, along with other evidence, has contributed to the belief that this is the cave where the great Greek tragedian withdrew to write his tragedies.

After Peristeria, the Faros (lighthouse) rises above the cape, which is the most southerly point of the island, and a little further along is the village of Kolones, nestling in the cove of a sandy bay.

On a raised area next to the village are cordoned off the remains of the prehistoric capital of the island, which was called either Salamis or Kychreia. This city was abandoned, whilst the other capital of Koulouri at Ambelakia was to flourish later. The area here took its name Kolones (columns) from the ruins.

The coastal road terminates a little to the north, at Saterli.

1. The little port at Kolones.
2. The view from the Ajax Club.
3. The beach at Kaki Vigla.

Moulki - Monastery of Ayios Nikolaos - Kanakia

At the final crossing before Salamis town (see the section on the Town of Salamis), the road to the left continues along the coast of the bay of Salamis in a south-westerly direction. A few metres after the crossing, the elegant building of the town hall can be spotted within a small park. Painted in a light yellow colour, with dark green door and window frames and white plaster decorative elements, it has all the features of a neo-classical building.

The first houses of the Moulki (Aianteio) become visible after six kilometres, gradually increasing in number until they form a small town which stretches out along the length of the beach and the slopes of the hill. Moulki is also a large summer resort, and this is why many of the houses are summer houses.

The road forks at Moulki. The branch to the left leads to Kaki Vigla, which we visited earlier, and the right-hand branch ascends the mountain that is thickly covered in pine trees, so thickly that they hide the view of the sea. Only at a clearing can you enjoy the panoramic view over the gulf of Salamis, with Moulki down below and the town of Salamis visible in the background.

After the upward slope begins the downward journey. The Monastery of Ayios Nikolaos Lemonion (St Nicholaos of the Lemons) appears further down in a gully. This was once a male monastery which was restored in 1742 (we do not know when it was founded) and which about 40 years ago became a female nunnery. Its cathedral church is a single-aisled basilica dating to the 17th century. Its location is most charming, with a spring, much greenery, and a brown precipice next to it. Opposite is the fine little 10th-century Byzantine church of Ayios Ioannis Kalyvitis. After the Monastery of Ayios Nikolaos the road descends to the sea, where the summer resort of Kanakia stretches out along the beach, with its small artificial harbour protecting a few small boats.

1. Ayios Nikolaos at Lemonia.
2. The beach at Kanakia.
3. Ayios Ioannis Kalyvitis.

AEGINA

Aegina, in the centre of the Argosaronic, immediately conquers the visitor. One can see this for oneself as soon as one confronts its enchanting port, with its crowd of colourful boats and the old houses along the pier. A walk around the town will lead to many historical buildings dating from the 19th century. Among them is the house of Capodistrias, the first Governor of Greece after the War of Independence in 1821. It has remained standing to remind us that Aegina was for two years the temporary capital city of Greece, before it was officially installed in Nafplion. A stroll near the port will bring the visitor to the archaeological site of Kolonas. Here where the ancient city was built, when Aegina, with its powerful fleet, ruled the seas, long before Athens began to make its presence felt.

Once the visitor has completed his or her trip around the town of Aegina, then the tour of the island will begin. At the foot of Oros, the tallest mountain on Aegina, he or she will 'discover' the sanctuary of Zeus Hellanios founded, according to the myth, by Aiakos, son of Zeus and grandfather of the heroes of the Trojan War Achilles and Ajax.

The visitor will discover the island's beautiful sands as he or she follows the coastal road southwards in the direction of the pretty fishing village of Perdikas. And he or she will be able to enjoy the indented coastline and the luscious-green northern coasts when travelling towards Souvala, the island's second port.

The route that will remain unforgettable, though, is the one which passes the Monastery of Ayios Nektarios and the medieval village of Palaiochora, to arrive at the famous Temple of Aphaia. Here, on a verdant hill on the north-eastern edge of the island, one can marvel at the temple that is considered to be the forerunner of the Parthenon.

The route ends below at the bay of Ayia Marina (St Marina), the island's largest summer resort with its beautiful sandy beach and calm waters.

Aegina is charming, with the mildest climate in the whole of Greece, many interesting sights and very good tourism facilities, offering the visitor a pleasant and eventful stay. And it has one further great advantage: it is only one hour by boat from the port of Piraeus.

The island of Aphaia

Geography

Aegina is the second largest island in the Argosaronic - the largest being Salamis - and it is located almost in the centre of the Saronic Gulf. It has an area of 85 square kilometres, a coastline of 57 kilometres, and is 16 nautical miles from Piraeus. The island has over 11,000 permanent residents, over half of whom live in the town of Aegina. The luscious-green little island of Angistri is 4 nautical miles to the south-west of the port of Aegina. Very close to Aegina's south-west edge is the small picturesque islet of Moni.

Local Produce

In the small valleys and plateaus of the island there are many areas covered in pistachio trees. The 'Aegina pistachio' is famed, and is the island's main produce. Other produce include raisins, olives and almonds.

Pottery is a tradition on Aegina. The porous walls of its clay jugs - kanata, as they are known in Greek - help to keep the water cool, and they were much in demand before the appearance of electric refrigerators. Only a few people work as potters today, making not only jugs, but all kinds of ceramic products.

AEGINA

Morphology

Aegina is shaped almost like an equilateral triangle, with each side having a length of nearly 12 kilometres. It has low mountain ranges, many of which are covered in pine forests. Its highest mountain is Oros, also known as Profitis Ilias, with an altitude of 532 metres. Its eastern and southern coasts are precipitous - with the exception of the large gulf of Ayia Marina - whilst the remaining coasts are flatter, with small and large gulfs. The climate is the mildest in all of Greece.

LEGEND

- Surfaced road
- Non-surfaced road
- Archaeological site
- Church
- Monastery
- Castle
- Beach
- Camp site

N

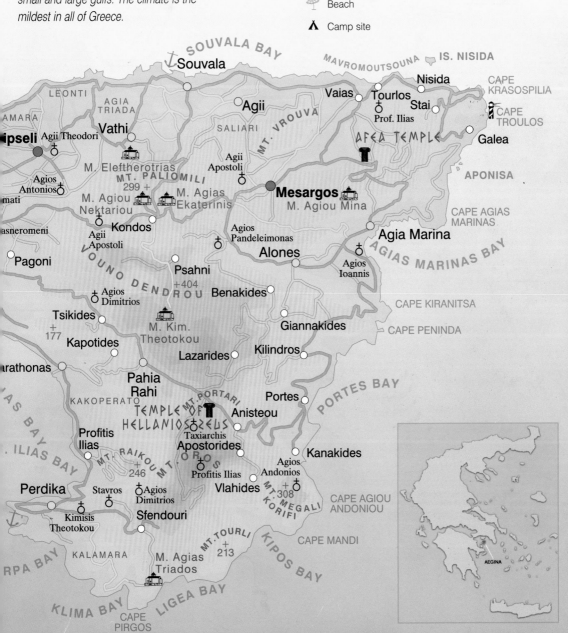

SOUVALA BAY

MAVROMOUTSOUNA — IS. NISIDA

Souvala

Nisida

CAPE KRASOSPILIA

LEONTI

AGIA TRIADA

Vaias — Tourlos — Stai

Prof. Ilias

CAPE TROULOS

AMARA

Agii

MT. VROUVA

SALIARI

AFEA TEMPLE

Galea

Ipseli

Agii Theodori

Vathi

Agii Apostoli

APONISA

Agios Antonios

M. Eleftherotrias

MT. PALIOMILI

299 +

M. Agias Ekaterinis

Mesargos

M. Agiou Mina

CAPE AGIAS MARINAS

mati

M. Agiou Nektariou

asneromeni

Kondos

Agii Apostoli

Agios Pandeleimonas

Agia Marina

Pagoni

VOUNO DENDROU

Psahni

Alones

Agios Ioannis

AGIAS MARINAS BAY

+404

Benakides

CAPE KIRANITSA

Agios Dimitrios

Giannakides

CAPE PENINDA

Tsikides

+177

M. Kim. Theotokou

Kapotides

Lazarides

Kilindros

arathonas

Pahia Rahi

MT. PORTARI

Portes

PORTES BAY

KAKOPERATO

TEMPLE OF HELLANIOS ZEUS

Anisteou

Profitis Ilias

Taxiarchis

Apostorides

Kanakides

MT. RAIKOU

MT. OROS

+246

Profitis Ilias

Agios Andonios

Perdika

Stavros

Agios Dimitrios

Vlahides

MT. 308

MT. MEGALI

KORIFI

CAPE AGIOU ANDONIOU

ILIAS BAY

Kimisis Theotokou

Sfendouri

RPA BAY

KALAMARA

M. Agias Triados

MT. TOURLI

+213

KIPOS BAY

CAPE MANDI

AEGINA

KLIMA BAY — LIGEA BAY

CAPE PIRGOS

MYTHOLOGY & HISTORY

Mythology

Aegina has a special place in Greek mythology as it is believed that it is from here that the generation of the heroes of the Trojan War began. It is said that the island took its name from the most beautiful of the twenty daughters of the river god Asopos. Zeus, first among the gods, fell in love with this girl, who was called Aegina. He secretly kidnapped her from her father and led her to the then deserted Saronic island of Oinoni or Oinopia (island of wine, oinos = wine). Here they had Aiakos together. Aiakos, as soon as he became King, changed the name of the island to Aegina in honour of his mother. But he found himself in a place which did not have a single soul, and was thus forced to ask for help from his father. Zeus transformed the ants (in Greek, myrmingia) of the island into people and granted them to Aiakos. The people who lived on the island were called Myrmidons, a name reminiscent of the word 'myrmingia.'

Aiakos had two sons with Endeis, Peleus and Telamon, and later, with, Psamanthi, Phokos. Aiakos' two eldest sons were jealous of their half-brother, who was better at athletic competitions than they. One day, in a stone-throwing competition, they killed him by throwing a stone over him. They left the island immediately, shocked and remorseful at their action. Peleus went to Thessaly and Telamon to the neighbouring island of Salamis, from where he desperately tried to contact his father and seek his forgiveness. Aiakos remained unrelenting and did not permit his son to return to the island. For this he gained the respect and admiration of the people and the gods, who made him a judge of the dead in Hades, along with Minos and Rhadamanthys.

This highly interesting section on the mythology of Aegina can be brought to a close with the birth of two of the heroes of the Trojan War: Achilles, son of Peleus and Thetis, and Ajax, son of Telamon and Eriboea.

1

2

History

3

Aegina was occupied in the later neolithic period (5th millennium BC), as we can see from the finds from the archaeological sites of Kolonas and Mesagros, near the Temple of Aphaia.

The first inhabitants came to the island from the coasts of the Peloponnese opposite. A second colonisation of the island took place in the 3rd millennium BC, this time by colonists from the Aegean. The Achaeans came to the island later (2000-1600 BC). It was then that the Aeginetans began to develop great naval and commercial activities and compete with the Minoans, who however succeeded in prevailing on the waters and in trade (1600-1200 BC). During the same period the Myrmidons, a people originating from Thessaly,

1. Byzantine well from the temple of Apollo
*   at the archaeological site of Kolones.*
2, 4. Views from the temple of Aphaia.
3. Vase representing the marriage of Thetis and Peleus,
*   ca 570 BC. Museum of Florence.*

Bust of Ioannis Capodistrias.

of Salamis (480 BC), putting up a fierce battle indeed. This fact was not enough to later prevent the Athenians, who had already grown into a great marine power, from occupying Aegina in 459 BC and forcing the island to pay a tribute. This was also the end of the island's peak period. The Athenians, at the beginning of the Peloponnesian War (431 BC), expelled the Aeginetans from the island and replaced them with what was known as a cleruchy, i.e. they settled the island with Athenians. The Aeginetans were returned to the island by the Spartans when the latter won the Peloponnesian War (in 404 BC).

Aegina came under the control of Pergamon for a period, and was later conquered by the Romans, who held it from 133 BC until the early Byzantine period in the mid-4th century AD. The centuries which passed were marked by foreign raids by Goths, Avars, etc. The most serious was the fierce attack of the Saracenes in the 9th century, which forced the residents of Kolonas to abandon their city and to build a new one, today's Palaiochora, in the centre of the island. This city, its many churches reminiscent of Mystras, experienced prosperity for several centuries.

The end of the long Byzantine period was signalled by the capture of Constantinople by the Franks (Western Europeans) in 1204. The 'Frangokratia,' period of Frankish rule, ensued on the island. Later came the 'Enetokratia' (Venetian rule), to be substituted twice by the 'Tourkokratia,' Turkish rule, which lasted until the War of Independence in 1821. The most significant event during the clashes between the Venetians and the Turks was the destruction of the island by the Turkish pirate Khair-ed-Din Barbarossa in 1537, and the raiding and pillaging by the Venetian Morosini in 1654.

Aegina played an important role during the struggle for freedom which began in 1821, and in 1828 it became the capital city of a free Greece. The first Governor, Ioannis Capodistrias, settled here in the Governor's House, or the Palace of Barba-Yiannis (Uncle John, in reference to Capodistrias), as the people called it. Here Capodistrias began the building of a new Greece. The visitor can see the Governor's House even today, along with all the other public works which survive on the island.

arrived on Aegina, settling in the area of Oros, the island's highest mountain. It is said that it was the Myrmidons who founded the sanctuary of Zeus Hellanios.

The Dorians arrived on Aegina around 950 BC, they were absorbed by the older residents and, all in common, they began once more to develop trade and shipping. There was continuous growth from this point on. Aegina was a member of the Kalaurian League (7th century BC), in which the fellow members were seven of the largest cities of ancient Greece, the centre of which was the sanctuary of Kalauria, today's Poros. Its ships travelled from the Black Sea to Egypt, shipping commercial goods. In order to conduct its commercial exchanges, Aegina was the first city in Greece to mint its own coins. These coins were silver and had a turtle on one side. Wonderful new buildings and sanctuaries were built at the city of Kolonas, whilst the arts flourished. Sculpture in particular did well, and the school of 'Aeginetan Art,' as it has been called, included top-rate sculptors.

In the period when Aegina was flourishing most, the danger of invasion by the Persians was real. Fearing that their involvement in the Persian War would lead to their commercial relations with Asia Minor being cut off completely, the Aeginetans initially decided not to support the other Greeks against the Persians. This did not much please the Athenians who, after the Greek victory at Marathon attempted, unsuccessfully, to overthrow the oligarchic regime of Aegina.

The Aeginetans eventually took part in the Battle

YESTERDAY & TODAY

The church of Ayios Nektarios at Palaiochora.

Sculpture - Architecture: *When talking about yesterday and today, we should certainly mention the ancient years, which gave Aegina such a rich cultural heritage. How can we not mention that the famous Aeginetan sculptors Kallon and Onatos, once they had finished carving the famous statues on the pediments of the Temple of Aphaia, helped - or so it is said - Pheidias in carving the Parthenon sculptures. It is also said that the technique used by these sculptors was a precursor for the creation of the Parthenon and of the shift from the archaic to the classical period.*

This was the 'Aeginetan Art,' which began in the archaic period and a leading figure of which was Smilis, a figure who is said to have been active in both Aegina and Samos and who may very well have been a mythical character. Smilis was followed by many brilliant artists, among them Kallon, creator of the west pediment of the Temple of Aphaia, and Onatos, creator of the later and finer east pediment of the Temple. Onatos was the last and also the greatest of the artists of the 'Aeginetan Workshop.'

The centuries passed, the ancient city of Aegina was abandoned, and the Aeginetans created Palaiochora, another Mystra with its Byzantine churches. Palaiochora was also abandoned in the 19th century, for the capital city to be transferred once more close to the sea, on the same site as before. Of course, this new town did not have anything in common with the old. It did not have its grand public buildings, there were no temples and famous sculptures. Even so, as far as architecture goes, 19th-century Aegina was pioneering, and it was from here that the neo-classical style began. The start was made in 1828 when Aegina became the capital of liberated Greece and the first Governor, Capodistrias, assisted by Greek and foreign architects, began to erect the first public buildings.

The imposing building of the Orphanage, with its simple Doric design, is considered as one of the first examples of the neo-classical style, and was subsequently repeated on other buildings in the town. This style later spread to Athens, and it became the dominant architectural style for a century. We will discuss the protected neo-classical buildings of Aegina town in more detail in the next section.

With the passing of time the official architecture of Aegina gave way to a popular architectural style, which on general lines can be considered as part of the broader 'Aegean Sea' style, yet with its own distinct character and particularities. The white of the villages of the Aegean has been replaced by soft and warm colours, which better match the idyllic environment of the island. This combination is today most noticeable in the town and port of Aegina.

Arts - Letters: *During this brief journey through yesterday and today, we should mention the great contribution of Aeginetans to the arts and letters. The contribution of the distinguished sculptors H. Kapralos (who was born in Agrinio but active in Aegina), N. Klonos and V. Antoniou; the painters F. Kappos, K. Galaris, Kontovrakis, and others; the photographer Y. Mairis; the historians and folklorists P. Ireiotis and Y. Kouliakourdis; the poets N. Lievas, A. Kyriakopoulos, A. Androutsos, K. Sarantakos and others; and the female poet T. Katsimingou-Yiannouli.*

Occupations: The Aeginetans may love the sea, but this does not mean that they were never engaged in **agriculture**, something which they are still involved in. The island has many cultivated areas, the use of which during wars and especially during the last centuries of the Tourkokratia was absolutely necessary. Aegina produces mainly olives, raisons, almonds, and, of course, pistachios, the cultivation of which started 100 years ago, for it to finally become the most profitable produce.

In addition to these main occupations - to which we must also add **sponge-diving**, which had disappeared by the mid-20th century - there were two other occupations on the island, which are also slowly disappearing. These are **pottery** and **lace-making**.

The first occupation is an ancient tradition on Aegina, continuing until our days. Indeed, in the years just before the Second World War, this trade had developed to such an extent that pottery was even exported. This was when the famous Aeginetan jugs with their colourful external decoration were produced. These jugs were in great demand, not just for storing water, but also because of their porous walls through which a small amount of water could seep and keep the outside of the jug damp. When this water evaporated, then, the walls of the jug were cooled thus keeping its contents cool as well. These jugs were usually placed on the sill of an open window. The results were both quicker and better using this method, whilst the elegant jugs on the window sills would add a note of charm to the little lanes.

The arrival of the electric refrigerator saw the end of the Aeginetan jugs. The '**kanatades**' - jug-makers - dwindled and today there remain only a few potters. And these potters no longer make jugs, but various ceramic wares to be sold to the tourists.

The art of **lace-making** was taught to the women of Aegina around 120 years ago by a foreign lady from western Europe. This technique was known as 'kopaneli' and was used to make table-cloths, doilies, centrepieces, etc. It is a finely-worked form of embroidery which demands much time and effort, and for this reason the product is quite pricey, making it difficult to sell. Perhaps this is the reason why there are only a few women still involved with 'kopanelia' today

Customs: *The passage of time and the closer relationship with Athens resulted in the local customs fading away or even dying out completely. The most important of the local customs, the wedding, however, still survives in various forms, mainly in the villages. It is a ritual which lasts for days.*

The wedding starts with the display of the bride's dowry, which is sprinkled with rice. The 'making of the bed' then follows, and the giving of gifts accompanied by songs and best wishes for the bride and the groom. The church service usually takes place on a Sunday, with the wedding feast in the evening, with musical instruments, dance and song. A feast which in the old days lasted for three days. The folk instruments which were used years ago at all the feasts and festivals were the violin, the lute and the dulcimer, whilst most of the songs that were heard were rhyming couplets, the lyric depending on the occasion. We have wedding songs such as the following:

"I'll sing you one song on the cherry tree
May the couple just brought together live long,
grow old."

We also have Easter carnival songs, feast songs, and songs of the sea which the Aeginetans call 'voyes' and which are of especial interest. These were the songs that were used to synchronise the pace at which oars were rowed, before they were replaced by engines, or the rhythm of the steps of the fishermen as they hauled at the trawl nets. So, we have the voya of the oar and the voya of the trawl net, such as this one by Yiannis Yiannitsaris:

'Yia lesa, yia lesa, let the trawl come in.
Yia lesa and it's getting dark
And the cauldron is boiling."

As for the **dances** *of Aegina, they are similar to other island dances, such as the group dance of the syrtos (especially 'The mountains of Palaiochora') and the ballo, danced by couples, as well as other dances, such as the sousta and the kalamatianos.*

The island's largest festival is on 15 August at the Monastery of the Chrysoleontissa, which attracts huge crowds. The largest religious gathering takes place on 9 November at the Monastery of Ayios Nektarios, when celebrations take place in memory of the Saint. This festival attracts the faithful not just from the island but from all over Greece.

The temple of Aphaia, 1820, painting by Hugh Williams.

THE TOWN OF AEGINA

As soon as the boat passes the lighthouse and archaeological site of Kolonas, on the north-west coast of the island, then the town and port of Aegina suddenly appear. The town, clambering up the green hills, and the port, with the long row of two- and three -storey houses in front of the dock. A crowd of all kinds of boats painted in all sorts of colours moored at the jetties rounds of this pretty picture.

The brilliant-white church of **Ayios Nikolaos Thalassinou** stands out at the entrance to the port,

on a wide jetty to the right. This church, with its two domes, is reminiscent of the Cyclades and is, we could say, the 'trademark' of Aegina. To the right, another jetty, narrower than the first, starts from the church of the Panayitsa, the imposing church on the right edge of the port. This jetty terminates at the kiosk of the Nautical Circle, opposite the church of Ayios Nikolaos. This point here, where the two jetties meet, is the entrance to the port.

The port of Aegina is wide, built on the site of the ancient commercial port. The ancient military harbour, as we shall see, is further to the north.

Views from the port of Aegina
and the little church of Ayios Nikolaos Thalassinos.

On the eastern side of the port there is another mole, where ferryboats and speed boats dock. This point is dominated by the large **mansion of Voyiatzis**, which has been described as a work of art, as have many other buildings. Opposite Voyiatzis' mansion, in the shadow of some large trees, is the square with the taxi and one-horse carriage rank. These are the carriages drawn along by one horse, dressed in multi-coloured costume.

These carriages are the traditional means of transport, a means which fits perfectly with the layout of the town and adds to its charm. Many people prefer the carriages to the taxis. Opposite the taxi rank is Eleftherias Square, near which is the mansion of Kanaris.

A walk along the waterfront is a delight. The wide coastal road, with much space for pedestrians to walk next to the sea, runs in both directions for wheeled vehicles, and for this reason there is a small dividing lane in the centre. On the side of the sea, the old buildings stand in a row with cafes, patisseries and shops on the ground floors, all competing with each other as to which is the most delightful. All have canopies laid out in front to protect the patrons from the sun, as well as the goods which are displayed on the pavement. Of course, among all these goods is the Aegina pistachio, the celebrated local produce, which only in Aegina do they know how to produce so well. Packaged in cellophane so as to protect the contents, it stands out either on its own or amongst the other products.

Somewhere in the middle of the port on the main road is the elegant neo-classical **Town Hall** building. Opposite this, in front of the sea, a unique, one might say, sight draws the attention of the visitor. This is an improvised fruit market set up on the caiques, which are loaded with various tasty fruits. Many of their crates are placed one next to the other on the dock, an extension of those already in the caiques.

1, 2. *The mansion of Kanaris in the square and the Voyiatzis mansion in the port have maintained their splendour over time.*

3. *The church of the Panayitsa.*

4, 5, 6. *Charming moments in the town.*

The south edge of the port is dominated, as we said, by the church of the Panayitsa. Next to it, inside a small park, is a marble statue of Capodistrias, the first Governor of Greece after the Revolution of 1821.

The rest of the town, particularly the centre, is also of great interest. Most of the tavernas are to be found on the first road parallel to the port, and on the second road parallel with Aphaias Street, an extension of Spyridon Roidis Street. The **Folk Museum** is also here, as well as the few remaining pottery shops, which sold the traditional clay jugs. Those which kept the water cool in the days when there were no fridges. Today, instead of jugs, they sell various ceramic wares.

Proceeding further into the town, we encounter the **Tower of Markellos** in an open space. This is a medieval building which was used by the first Greek government after the Revolution of 1821. Near this Tower there is yet another building, of great importance for modern Greek history. This is the **Government House**, the house of Capodistrias, the first Governor of a free Greece, from which he governed the country for two years after its independence, when Aegina was the temporary capital of Greece.

Next to the house of Capodistrias is the **Public Library**. A little to the south is the **Metropolitan Church**, an old church with three red domes and three large arches over its facade, upon which the roof of the forecourt is supported. To the south-west of the centre of the town, behind a football pitch, there stands a large building. This is the **orphanage**, built during Capodistrias' rule, which functioned both as a home and a school for orphans.

Public services were housed in this building, and it was then converted into a prison, which later closed. So, today it stands empty, awaiting its next use. Faneromenis Street, which passes along the Orphanage, proceeds towards the Monastery of the Faneromeni, where there is a semi-dilapidated 13th-century church and two smaller churches. To the south of the city, near the cemetery, there is another 19th-century mansion. This belonged to Harilaos Trikoupis, one of the great Greek prime ministers of the later 19th century.

The cathedral church of the Ayii Theodorii (SS Theodore), the so-called '**Beautiful Church**,' is located to the east of the town, near the neighbourhood of the Ayii Asomati and at a distance of around 2 km. from the port. It is perhaps the most important surviving church of Aegina, built in the late 13th century. Its interior is full of well-preserved wall paintings.

1. *The tower of Markellos.*
2. *The town hall.*
3. *The house of Harilaos Trikoupis.*
4. *The Governor's house, otherwise the house of Capodistrias.*
5. *The Metropolitan church.*

3

4

5

After Eleftherias Square, the coastal road proceeds in a north-west direction and passes the coast of Avra. Some say that this is where the military harbour of ancient Aegina was, although according to others it was located at the next bay. The ancient military harbour was excellently organised, with very good installations which it is said could hold as many as sixty triremes. Immediately after this coast and behind a small park is the hill with the archaeological site of Kolonas and the Museum (see below). The sandy beach of Kolonas stretches out behind the archaeological site, and this beach is the most busy of all those near the town.

The coastal road continues to the neighbour-hood of Plakakia, with its beautiful villas, amongst which stand out the Zaimis Tower and the Benizelos house within a large garden with palm trees.

After the Zaimis Tower the road continues along the north-west edge of Aegina, with its picturesque lighthouse and the little church of the Ayii Apostoli (Holy Apostles). The austere and simple house in which **Nikos Kazantzakis** - the internationally-acclaimed Greek novelist upon whose book 'The Life and Times of Alexis Zorbas' the film 'Zorba the Greek' was based - lived is a little past the lighthouse. The **Kapralos Museum** is a short distance from Kazantzakis' house. The great sculptor's works, dating from 1963 until his death in 1993, are exhibited here. It is said that the large sculpture entitled '**Mother**' and situated outside the museum next to the sea represents the artist's own peasant mother.

1. Kazantzakis' house.
2. The Kapralos mansion.
3. The tower of Zaimis, or of the Benizeli.
4, 5. The archaeological site at Kolonas
    and exhibits from the museum.

The archaeological site of Kolonas

This is a very important archaeological site, not simply because of the ruins of the famous temple of Apollo and other buildings, but because it contains the remains of ten successive prehistoric settlements dating from the late neolithic period (5th millennium BC) until the Mycenean period (1600-1200 BC).

All the finds are gathered on a hill to the north of the port, at the peak of which stands a single column (kolona), from which the hill took its name. The column, which is part of the temple of Apollo, is the only one which has remained upright of the eleven which stood on each of the long sides and the six on each of the short sides. The temple was built in the late 6th century BC and dominated the region due to its size and its beauty which was equal, it is said, to that of the Temple of Aphaia, which we shall see below. The foundations of some other structures belonging to the temple have also survived, such as the altar to the east of the temple, the Temple of Artemis to the south-east, two small rectangular buildings and a circular one.

There are also the remains of many walls from different eras, such as the Bronze Age fortress walls, the archaic acropolis walls, the Roman sanctuary walls, and the so-called port walls which run down towards the port. Other significant remains are those of a rectangular structure which was perhaps used as a gathering place and which Pindar refers to as a viewing gallery.

4

5

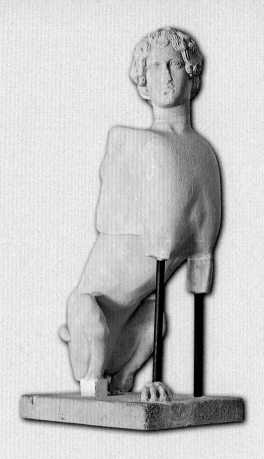

Exhibits from the museum of Kolonas.

The Museum of Kolonas

The Museum of Kolonas is located in front of the site in a new, square, one-storey building with a large atrium in the centre. The atrium contains sculptures from the cemetery of Reneia, from the time that Capodistrias brought them to Aegina. The splendid large and narrow hall of the museum contains some fine exhibits dating from the late neolithic period until the Roman period.

Among the finds are red-buff vases with painted decoration and small clay idols from the earliest prehistoric settlement (5th millennium BC), Bronze Age pottery (3rd millennium BC), such as the 'gravy boats' which stand out for their perfect technique, as well as Middle Bronze Age (2000 - 1600 BC) items, such as buff-grey painted vases and other Minoan-type vases. There are a large number of pottery items from the Mycenean period, whilst the archaic (7th - 6th century BC) vases are important too, such as the Ram

Jug representing Odysseus and his companions escaping from the Cyclops.

The archaic and early classical periods are also represented by the famous marble sphinx of Aegina (460 BC) as well as sculptures from the pediment of the Temple of Apollo. The sculpture of Herakles is most probably from the pediment of the earlier limestone temple, whilst the tombstone with relief sculpture dates to the late 5th century.

At the entrance to the museum are the impressive models of a house from the prehistoric city III on the hill of Kolonas, the so-called 'white house,' and of a bronze-foundry. The models make quite clear that the 'white house' had two floors. The foundry dates to around 2300 BC, whilst the 'white house' dates to around 2200 BC.

TOUR OF THE ISLAND

Kypseli - Souvala - Vaia

This route mainly covers the northern edge of the island, which is the most densely-populated. From the house of Kazantzakis and the Kapralos Museum the road continues for Souvala. This is the quickest route from the town of Aegina, and goes to Souvala via Kypseli, the island's second-largest town which is almost merged with the capital.

The brilliant-white old domed church of **Ayios Moulos** can be seen from afar between this road and the coastal one, set on a verdant height.

The large, pretty square of Kypseli, dominated by the beautiful church of the Evangelismos (when the Archangel Gabriel told Mary that she was going to give birth to the Son of God), is about 4 km. from the town of Aegina. The road continues for the village of Vathy and then descends to reach, after another 4 km., Souvala, the harbour of Vathy and the island's second port. Souvala is known for its hot springs which can help with arthritis, rheumatism, skin problems and gynaecological problems. It is also a tourist centre and there are regular direct connections with Piraeus. The large docks, with the fishermen's nets spread out and the plethora of fishing and tourist boats impress. There are hotels, and many apartments and rented rooms to meet the needs of visitors.

A very interesting trip can be made from *Souvala*. This goes up to Palaiochora and the Monastery of Ayios Nektarios, and meets the central arterial road from Aegina through Aphaia and Ayia Marina, which we shall read more about below. The coastal road continues in an easterly direction

1

2 *and passes alongside the luscious-green Ayii,
to reach, after 3.5 km., Vaia, yet another small
tourist resort, smaller than Souvala, with a pretty
little port.*

*From **Vaia**, as from Souvala, a road rises
towards Mesagros and the central arterial road of
Aegina-Aphaia-Ayia Marina*

3

1. *The central square with the church of the
   Evangelismos at Kypseli.*
2. *Ayios Nikolaos Moulos at Kypseli.*
3. *The little port at Vaia.*
4. *The port at Souvala.*

4

Ayios Nektarios Monastery
Palaiochora
Chrysoleontissa Monastery

This route is the first section of the one of the largest and most important routes throughout the island. You can start from Aphaias Street, which begins at the centre of the port and which is the second parallel road with the port. You can also start on this route from other roads further to the south, which all finally meet up with Aphaias Street.

The road cuts across the town of Aegina and continues in an easterly direction towards the island's hinterland. The houses become sparser and sparser, to be replaced by fields with beautiful country churches and lots of greenery. The nature here is serene, with nothing out of the ordinary, and the smooth lines of the mountains create an atmosphere of calm. Yet, the first surprise comes after a distance of about 5.5 km. An imposing church with two tall belfries and four

rows of windows with red arches, suddenly appears on the left of the road. This is **Ayios Nektarios**, a new church built below the Monastery of Ayios Nektarios, the architecture of which is reminiscent of that of Ayia Sophia in Constantinople. This nunnery, the entrance to which is on the road for Souvala and very near to the crossing with the Aegina-Aphaia arterial route, was built at the beginning of the 20th century on the site of a small Byzantine monastery dedicated to the Zoodochos Pigi (life-giving source) by the Bishop of Pentapoli Nektarios. Ayios Nektarios passed the last years of his life in the monastery, carrying out a great philanthropical work and gaining the admiration and adoration of the faithful, who flocked to the monastery to meet him.

Many still talk about his generosity and his ability to cure people suffering from incurable diseases. Ayios Nektarios died in 1920 and was buried in the monastery. He was canonised in 1961. From then

The Monastery of Ayios Nektarios at Palaiochora.

Aerial photograph. Souvala and Kypseli can be seen.

Icon of Ayios Nektarios.

on the monastery, which had been known as the Monastery of Ayios Theodoros, was renamed the Monastery of Ayios Nektarios. The Saint's memory is celebrated on 9 November, when thousands of faithful gather at the monastery, having come from all parts of Greece.

On the right of the road which goes from the church of Ayios Nektarios to Souvala, and before the entrance to the Monastery, is the small, brilliant-white **nunnery of Ayia Aikaterini**, surrounded by vegetation, the tall cypress trees standing out. This same road, as it ascends, winds around a rocky hill on its right. Some grey-yellow buildings can be seen scattered around on this hill. These are the approximately 35 of the many churches that existed in Palaiochora (tradition says there were 365) which remain standing. Around 20 of these still have some fine wall-paintings preserved.

Palaiochora is another Mystras. It began to be built in 896 after a fierce raid by Saracene pirates on the coastal town of Aegina. Centuries later it became the capital of the island, to be abandoned at the beginning of the 19th century when the inhabitants slowly began to return to the sea and rebuild the new Aegina.

The ruins of **Palaiochora** are approached from a

pass in the hills, there where the ascent of the road towards Souvala ends. At this point is the church of Stavros, the first church which the visitor to Palaiochora will meet.

From here the footpaths which follow the old paved roads lead to the old Byzantine churches, such as Panayia Yiannouli and Ayios Georgios the Catholic. During the period of Catalan rule this church belonged to the Catholics, but was later again restored to the Orthodox. Other churches include Episkopi, the metropolitan church of Palaiochora, in which the Bishop of Aegina Dionysius, later saint of Zakynthos, officiated (his cell is preserved next to the church), the Taxiarchis (Archangel), a cruciform church, the Ayii Theodori, etc.

After Episkopi, a diversion to the left from the main path leads, after an uphill walk for fifteen minutes, to the Kastro, the castle, built by the Venetians in the 17th century. At the peak there are preserved two small churches, built next to each other. These are Ayios Georgios and Ayios Dimitrios. There are the ruins of walls, houses and wells on the **Kastro**, and the view from here, especially towards the beach of Souvala, is exceptional.

After the visit Palaiochora, you can continue your route on the main road towards Aphaia and Ayia Marina, or go in a northerly direction towards Souvala. There is yet another road in a southerly direction, leading from the new church of Ayios Nektarios in the hamlet of Kontos. This road is three kilometres long and provides the opportunity for a visit to the important **Monastery of the Chrysoleontissa**. The monastery is located in the centre of the island, and it dominates from high up on the luscious-green mountain slopes. The road terminates at a mountain range, from which point we can reach the monastery after a walk of about fifteen minutes.

The monastery, with tall fortress-like walls, was built at the beginning of the 17th century so that the old monastery at Leonti on the north coast of the island could be moved to a safer place and escape from the relentless pirate raids. It is a large two-storey building with a courtyard in the centre. In the courtyard there is a church and, next to it, a tall three-storey tower. The church is newer and was built on the site of the older one, which was

destroyed in a fire. The icon of the Panayia (Virgin Mary) is well-worth seeing. The Aeginitans all bow with respect to this icon. The church's iconostasis and wall-paintings are also of interest. The Monastery, which celebrates its feast day on 15 August, when the island's largest festival takes place, converted in 1935 from a male monastery to a female nunnery.

1. Palaiochora.
2. The Ayii Theodori, or the Beautiful Church.
3. The Monastery of Ayia Aikaterini.
4. Panayia Chrysoleontissa.
5. The Bishop's residence at Palaiochora.

Mesagros - Aphaia - Ayia Marina

The road from Ayios Nektarios leads in an easterly direction, nine miles from the town of Aegina, to Mesagros, a large hamlet with a few houses and whose inhabitants work in agriculture. The surrounding area has quite a bit of vegetation, including, of course, plenty of pistachios.

After Mesagros begins the ascent up a beautiful pine-clad hill, at the top of which is one of the most beautiful temples of ancient Greece, the Temple of Aphaia. It was not by chance that this spot was chosen as the location of the temple. The panoramic view from here over the charming gulf of Ayia Marina is outstanding. Moreover, traces of a later neolithic (3000 BC) settlement have been found. This settlement and Kolona are the oldest settlements on the island.

Before the temple that we see today was built, two smaller temples had been constructed. The first was built in around 600 BC and only a small section of its foundations survive. Only the altar survives from the second temple. The third temple to have been built, the one we see today, is an exceptional example of late archaic architecture. It is in the Doric order and was built with local limestone in around 500 BC. It had six columns on the short sides and twelve on the long sides.

Twenty of these columns survive today, whilst in the cella (the main area of the temple) there were two internal colonnades parallel to the main colonnades, with five columns each. There was a second row of five smaller columns above, built in such a way as to form a stoa, in the form of a raised section around the three sides of the temple. The decoration on both the exterior as well as the interior was exceptional. What gave the temple its greatest splendour, however, were its famous pedimental sculptures. Unfortunately, however, these have suffered a similar fate to those of the Parthenon.

The temple of Aphaia.

In 1811 the German Baron von Hallerstein and the English architect Cockerell, who discovered the sculptures after excavation, transported them to Zakynthos, which was then under British rule, and from there they went to Italy. They were then bought in an auction by Ludwig I, King of Bavaria, father of the future King of Greece Otto, who took them to the Glypthotek in Munich, where they remain. These sculptures include 16 statues carved from Parian marble and many other pieces.

These sculptures formed scenes from the Trojan War, with the goddess Athena as the central figure in both the pediments. As a result, it was initially believed that the temple had been built in honour of Athena. During excavations carried out much later (in 1901), the German archaeologist Fürtwangler discovered an ancient description with the name of Aphaia. She was a local goddess, and tradition associates her with the Cretan Britomartis. According to the myth, Britomartis was the daughter of Zeus and half-sister of Artemis, who loved her greatly and took her hunting with her. Minos fell madly in love with Britomartis, and she sought refuge in the sea. As she jumped into the waters, her foot was caught up in the nets of some fishermen, who transported her to Aegina. Her misfortunes were not to end here, though, as a fisherman tried to rape her. Artemis then intervened, and made Britomartis invisible and took her into the island's woods. In this way, then, Britomartis became 'aphanis,' or invisible. In the dialect of the time, this was pronounced 'aphaia.'

A section of the eastern pediment was destroyed a few years after the erection of the building. The shattered statues were buried, as was customary, and new ones put in their place. Thankfully, Fürtwangler was able to uncover them, so that the National Archaeological Museum in Athens could

1. View from the temple of Aphaia.
2. The gulf of Ayia Marina.

1

also have a piece, even a little one, of the famous sculptures of the Temple of Aphaia.

Around the temple there are the remains of various buildings. Entrance to the archaeological site is through a small gateway. Straight ahead to the right are the ruins of the priests' houses and immediately after them are the baths. There follow the great gate and the path taken by the procession, beginning from the altar and reaching the entrance to the temple, which is in its east side. The temple was divided, as was the rule, into the pronaos, the cella - the main area of the temple which housed the goddess's statue - and the opisthodomos at the back.

The Temple of Aphaia is connected with the port of Aegina, 11.5 km. away, by coaches which depart from Ayia Marina. The archaeological site is open every day, except Mondays, from 8:30 to 17:00.

From Aphaia, the road descends with many bends, to reach the pretty gulf of Ayia Marina after 4 kilometres. This was once a fishing village with two or three tavernas, but has today grown, thanks to its wonderful sands and dense pine forest, into a large tourist centre which in the summer bustles with life. Villas, hotels, restaurants, bars, an organised beach with facilities for water sports, and anything else the visitor could ask for, they will surely find in this resort.

The little harbour is full of boats small and large, whilst in the summer there are direct connections with Piraeus in small boats. From Ayia Marina the road, following the coast, continues on to the fishing port of Portes. The return journey to the town of Aegina can be made through the settlement of Alones, with its small villas and restaurants, via a road which meets the main road at Mesagros, by-passing Aphaia.

2

Pacheia Rachi
Temple of Zeus Hellanios - Portes

This is another route of great interest, centring on an archaeological site that is directly connected with the mythology and history of Aegina. This route crosses the island from north-west to south-east, passing alongside Oros, Aegina's highest mountain. The road - Faneromenis Street - begins at the old prisons of Aegina and at first travels parallel with the coastal road. It turns left to Pacheia Rachi before meeting with the coastal road.

As this road ascends the view on the right over the sea becomes all the more beautiful. At first you can see the town of Aegina in the distance as it is left behind, whilst to the left is Angistri, luscious green and also in the distance. The islet of Moni soon appears before the peninsula of Methana. A little further to the left, like a white line on a narrow strip of land which continues into the sea, is picturesque Perdika. The row of white houses on the beach down below belong to the village of Marathon. We shall have the chance to see all these from closer up on the last leg of our journey around the island.

*The village of **Pacheia Rachi,** which looks out over the sea and the plain, soon appears. The belfry and blue dome of the church stand out. Just beyond the village are the new facilities of the Centre for the Care of Wild Animals and Birds, which is being relocated here from the former prisons of Aegina. Every year the Centre takes care of many wounded (mainly by hunters) and sick wild animals and birds. The Centre is a very commendable effort by a group of young people whose aim is to care for these animals and then to return them to their natural environment.*

*Beyond the Centre, a dirt road to the right leads to Sfyricthres, and the archaeological site with the **sanctuary of Zeus Hellanios**. From a distance one can discern the broad, grand stone staircase next to a Hellenistic wall.*

On the upper part of the staircase, to the left, is the Byzantine church of the Taxiarches, the Archangels, which used to be the cathedral church of a monastery. The ruins of the monks' cells

4 can still be seen round about the church. The wall was most probably built in order to fill it in so as to create a large, flat, square area upon which the sanctuary of Zeus Hellanios was built.

Tradition has it that no rain fell on Aegina for many years, and the island suffered greatly. Aiakos, the mythical King of Aegina and son of Zeus, was advised by the oracle at Delphi to plead with his father to bring rainfall. His plea was heard and, in order to thank Zeus, Aiakos built this temple in the god's honour and established his cult here.

Today, from the south-east corner of this large
5 terrace, and beneath some tall rocks, we can see the foundations of a large structure and the bases of three rows of columns, which supported the roof. It is likely that this structure acted as a hostel for pilgrims. Further up, at a little distance from the terrace, there are two wells within the rocks and the large stones, which most likely were also created to serve the needs of the pilgrims. These wells, most likely fed by some spring, even today contain a little stagnant water, which is not, however, drinkable.

Above the temple stands the mountain with the ancient name of Oros, and which is directly associated with the cult of Zeus on the island. It has the shape of a cone and is covered in rocks and stones. The footpath leading up to its peak (532 m), the tallest in Aegina, is to the west. Traces of buildings have been found on the peak, and it was initially believed that they were part of the sanctuary of Zeus Hellanios. This is not the case, however, as these buildings date to the 13th century BC whilst it appears that the Dorians brought the cult of Zeus to Aegina in around 1000 BC.

The view of the island and the whole of the Argosaronic from the peak of Mt Oros, today known as Profitis Ilias, is splendid. The small, brilliant-white church which stands here is not dedicated, as is usually the case, to the Prophet Elias but to the Analapsi, the Ascension of Christ.

1. The village of Pacheia Rachi.
2, 4. Views from the temple of Zeus Hellanios.
3. The holy mountain Oros.
5. The church of the Archangels from the temple of Zeus Hellanios.

From the crossing with the dirt road that leads to the sanctuary of Zeus Hellanios, the central road continues towards the east and soon starts to descend down to the sea, with many bends. There is much vegetation along this route, mainly pine and olive trees. A little house to the right of the road catches the eye. This is, in fact, an azure, two-storey mill with a conical blue roof. At the end of the road lies the isolated and serene fishing village of Portes, with its few houses and little taverna built on a rise. A beautiful pebbly beach stretches out to the right, whilst to the left, next to the road which leads to the north, is the small artificial harbour which protects the boats in the area.

This same road continues alongside the pretty villages, finally ending up at Ayia Marina, which we discussed in the previous route.

1. Perdika and the island of Moni.
2, 4. The beach and the mill-cum-home at Portes.
3. The beaches between Portes and Ayia Marina.

Marathon - Perdika

The route taken to reach Perdika is idyllic and peaceful, not at all like the others we have covered so far. The road, which follows the coast with almost no bends at all, proceeds alongside the neo-classical villas near to the port of Faros. From here on, it continues alongside the coast of the gulf of Marathon. This is the open gulf in which the Greek war ships gathered after their victory at Salamis in order to divide the spoils. It is also the gulf at which Capodistrias, the first governor of Greece after the Revolution of 1821, disembarked in order to set up his first government. The **village of Marathon** appears after a total of 4 kilometres from the port of Aegina. Marathon has an organised beach and has developed into a tourist resort. From here on, the houses become fewer and fewer. There is a small strip of land in between the road and the coast, which has a fair covering of greenery. Eucalyptus trees, with their tall and slender trunks, bushes, reeds, and behind all this lies the sea, peaceful, alight, with an amazing blue colour, the shades of which fluctuate as the distance from the coast increases.

Further in the distance, on a bare, long and narrow peninsula, the white houses of **Perdika** shine in the light of the sun. Moni, the conical-shaped islet, stands out to the right, and behind all this, the sharp dark grey-blue peaks of the Methana mountain range.

A little before Perdika, the organised beach of **Aiginitissa**, with its beautiful sands and green surroundings, most definitely attracts the visitor's eye. At this point the road ascends, now entering the infertile earth of Perdika. Yet, even in this treeless place, which is watered on both sides by the sea, a surprise awaits the visitor. On the southern side of the peninsula there is a charming fishing village which, despite its tourist development, has managed to preserve all the features of the Aegean Sea which characterised it of old. Its port, full of colourful fishing caiques and other boats, buzzes with life. The raised road above the port, with the tavernas all in a row on one side and the little tables set up along the seafront on the other, remains just as it was many years ago. A few small hotels and rented rooms have, of course, now been added. The place has been noticeably developed, the large church of Ayios Sozos, which celebrates its feast day on 7 September with a large festival in the

1. The beach of Aiginitissa.
2, 3. Views from the fishing village of Perdika.

village, built. Yet, the village's charm is still the same. The visitor coming from the town of Aegina (9 km. away) will enjoy walking through the village lanes, with their old houses and gardens full of flowers, as well as trying some fresh fish - something never absent from Perdika.

The visitor can even, if it is the right season, visit the islet of **Moni** opposite, and enjoy a wonderful swim in its fantastically-clean waters. It is only a short distance away, and there are regular connections throughout the summer months.

You disembark at a small, organised sandy beach on a cove on the north coast of the islet. A beautiful forest stretches out beyond the beach, clambering up the slope of a steep mountain and covering almost the whole of the northern area of Moni. The rest of the islet is bare and craggy, with rocks at its highest point, which tapers off into a cone. The island belongs to the Greek Travellers' Club, and rare species of animals are nurtured on it, such as the chamois goat-antelope (the Cretan kri-kri) and peacocks.

From Perdika, a relatively new road leading to the east goes to the village of Sfentouri, on the north slope of Mt Oros (Profitis Ilias).

ANGISTRI

From the port of Aegina, it appears like a dark-green stroke of paint over the blue sea of the Saronic Gulf. The little island of Angistri is so full of pine trees that in antiquity it was called Pityousa, from pitys, a pine-bearing tree today known as koukounaria ('pine cone'). The ancients also called the island Kekryfaleia, a name mentioned by Homer, who tells us that during the Trojan War it was allied with Aegina. The archaeological finds from the island indicate that it was inhabited by at least 500 BC.

Angistri lies around 3.5 nautical miles to the west of Aegina, and 22 nautical miles south-west of Piraeus. It has an area of 13 square kilometres, the largest part of which is covered in pine forests, olive groves, almond and fig trees. The ferryboats coming from Aegina and Piraeus moor at **Skala**, the natural harbour on the north-east coast of the island. This is also where most people come, and there are many hotels and tavernas to serve the needs of visitors. The large, brilliant-white church of the **Ayii Anargyri**, which dominates the port and is visible from quite a distance away, is impressive. The church celebrates its feast day on 1 July, when there is a great fair.

2. Little lane at Mylos.

1. Skala, with the brilliant white church of the Ayii Anargyri.

3. The little port at Skala.

The beach of Halkiada at Angistri.

The islet of Aponisos.

Above Skala, on the slopes of the mountain, is the village of **Metochi**, with a panoramic view over the beach and the sea. A coastal road leading from Skala in a south-westerly direction, passes first by the beach of Skliri and terminates at the pebbly beach of Halkida.

Again from Skala, the central coastal road in the opposite direction (to the west) leads after 2 kilometres to **Mylos**, or, as it was later named, Megalochori (Big Village). This is the island's largest village and also its capital. There is a harbour here at which the small boats which service local connections mainly moor (there is a marina), and there is also a pebbly beach for swimming. Megalochori and Skala share between them the island's hotels, rented rooms and tavernas. The metropolitan church of Megalochori is the Zoodochos Pigi, which celebrates its feast day on Easter Sunday.

From the raised area above the harbour of Megalochori, which is on the north edge of the island, the road turns now towards the south, following the coast but this time from above and at a distance from the coast. Within the thick forests, the beautiful bays with the azure waters begin to make their appearance. One of these is the lovely beach of Dragonara, which can be reached via a little turning to the right.

After a total of five kilometres from Mylos, the road terminates at Limenaria, the island's fourth village. Here, there is a handful of tavernas and the church of Ayia Kyriaki, which celebrates its feast day on 7 July, when there is a great fair. The route from Metochi to Skala, Mylos and Limenaria is serviced by a local bus. Turning once more, this time in a westerly direction, the road from Limenaria leads to a strange landscape with a singular beauty. Before reaching the coast, the road passes a small harbour and finally terminates at the sea, opposite the islet of **Aponiso** which lies next to Angistri. Further beyond is the larger islet of Dorousa which, along with the area's other sights, creates a picture of exceptional splendour.

Angistri, with its beautiful, primitive nature, good tourism facilities, the water sports and nightlife it has to offer the young, and, foremost, its beautiful, clean beaches, is a most attractive option which will continue to attract an ever-increasing number of visitors.

The beach at Skliri (right).

POROS

The island of Poseidon

Mother Nature put all of her skills to use when she created this place. She placed it next to the coast of the Peloponnese, leaving a narrow pass between the two coasts. A pass just like a broad, azure river which proceeds like a snake, forcing the boat to twist and turn in order to navigate. And once she had placed it here, Nature filled the island with pine trees, sprouting from its peak and leading down all the way to the sea. She even planted a lemon forest on the coast of the Peloponnese opposite, so that the aroma from the buds of the lemon trees would travel here in the spring. When Poseidon saw the island, he became jealous. It belonged to Apollo, and in order to make it his he had to exchange it for Delphi and Delos. When the people saw it, they were dazzled by its beauty and so built a beautiful city on a hill, at the narrowest point of the channel.

And thus myth blends with reality - because this city indeed exists, and is only 2 1/2 hours by boat

from Piraeus. The verdant island is there, next to the Peloponnese, and it awaits its visitors to show
them around. To take them through the lanes of the town and up to the peak of the hill with the clock,
so they can marvel at the view over the channel from up there. Next it will take them to its beautiful
sandy beaches, Neorio on one side and Askeli on the other. The visitors will be charmed by the
beauty of the sea, the tavernas and the new hotels. They will swim in the wonderfully-clean waters
and in the early evening they will visit the celebrated church of the Zoodochos Pigi, which looks out
over the sea from high above. And when they have seen all this and ask to learn more about
Poseidon, then the island will lead them up a surfaced road high up in the wooded mountain to show
them the ruins of a temple. This will be the famed temple of Poseidon, where the seat of the alliance
of the seven most powerful city-states of antiquity was. Something akin to Brussels, the seat
of the European Union today.

POROS

LEGEND

Surfaced road
Non-surfaced road
Archaeological site
Church
Monastery
Castle
Beach
Camp site

MT. VOUNOKORI
+154

VARIARNIA BAY

+15

CAPE AKRITSA

FOUSA
POSIDONOS
TEMPLE

+185

MT. KAMARA
+273

Agios
Nektarios

CAPE NEDA

IS. DASKALIO

MEGA NERIO BAY

Megalo
Neorio

MT. VPROFITIS ILIAS

Mikro
Neorio

Askeli

KANALI

MONASTIRI BAY

N

POROS

SFERIA

Geography

AHERDO

Poros is located on the western side of the entrance to the Saronic Gulf, very close to the Peloponnesian coast. It has an area of 33 square kilometres, a coastal length of 32 kilometres, and is 31 nautical miles from Piraeus. It has a permanent population of 3,500 residents, the majority of whom live in the town of Poros. The rest live in the coastal settlements, especially the resorts, which have developed to the east and west of Poros town.

IS. BISTI

Morphology

All the island's hills are covered in thick pine forest. Notable hills are Profitis Ilias (314 m.) in the centre of the island and Vigla (390 m.) to the east, the island's tallest hill. In contrast with the greater part of the island, there is a small rocky, volcanic peninsula in the south, with a channel in its narrow neck. This is Sfairia, which resulted from the eruption of the neighbouring volcano of Methana in 273 BC. The town of Poros is today built on this peninsula, whilst the main island is the Kalavria of antiquity. The island's only valley, Fousa, is in the north and is fairly fertile, with mainly vine groves.

GONIA BAY

MAKRI AVLAKI BAY

CAPE KOKORELI

CAPE KOKORELI

MT. VIGLA
+
358

MT. SKALA MODI

MT. KOKORELI

IS. MODI

HI

M. Zoodohou Pigis

MYTHOLOGY & HISTORY

Mythology

Mythology has it that Kalavria once belonged to Apollo. Because, however, Poseidon, god of the sea, was so persistent in asking for it, Apollo decided to exchange it. He gave Kalavria to Poseidon, taking Delphi and Delos from him.

Kalavria, especially the little islet of Sfairia right by it, is connected in Greek mythology with the birth of Theseus, the most important Attic hero. It is therefore natural that the myth of Theseus should be one of the most interesting.

Theseus, following his mother's orders, moves the rock and finds the sandals and sword of Aegeus (Roman copy, 1st century AD, London, British Museum).

son who was strong enough to move the rock, then he should take the sandals and the sword and come and find him in Athens.

Aethra gave birth to a son, to Theseus, who passed his childhood in the court of Pytheas. It is said that when Theseus was seven-years-old Herakles came to the palace. As Herakles was about to remove his lion-skin, all the children of the nobles ran away scared, thinking it was a real lion.

Theseus, however, instead of running away picked up a club to hit the

Opposite Kalavria was Troezen. The King here was Pytheas, son of Pelops who gave his name to the Peloponnese. Pytheas had a daughter who, like the light of the moon, was called Aethra.

In between Troezen and Kalavria there was a small islet, Sfairia, there where the town of Poros is today built. This islet was dedicated to the goddess Athena, to whom the virgins of Troezen dedicated their bridal belts before marrying.

One day Aethra went to Sfairia, and here she met Aegeus, the King of Athens, with whom she spent the night. In the morning, before leaving for Athens, Aegeus laid his sandals and sword on the ground and rolled a rock over them. He told Aethra that if she gave birth to a

beast with. When he was sixteen-years-old Theseus pushed away the rock, put on the sandals, picked up the sword and, full of strength and power, started off to meet his father in Athens. On the road for Athens, he succeeded at his first great labours, which were almost equal to the labours of Herakles.

In Greek mythology, it is believed that the sea of Poros was the home of Skylla, a sea creature who filled sailors with fear.

Three points are associated with the name of this mythological creature: the cape of Skylaio, the easternmost in the Peloponnese, at a little distance to the south-east of Poros, one of the Tselevinia islands which is called Skyli, and the popular Poros beach of Askeli, the name of which is possibly linked to the word Skylla.

History

Poros, as can be ascertained from the finds in the area of the temple of Poseidon, was occupied from neolithic times. An Early Helladic settlement developed later in the same area, which subsequently gave its place to newer settlements in the Mycenean and later periods. The remains of the ancient city of Kalavria have yet to be found. By contrast, the ruins of a second city, the harbour of Kalavria, are located on the bed of the sea at the bay of Vagionia to the south. These ruins are visible when the waters are calm.

Although the ruins of the ancient city of Kalavria have not been found, the foundations of the famed temple of Poseidon and of seven auxiliary buildings, described in the section on the tour of the island (see Temple of Poseidon - Vagionia) have, thankfully, been found. These were uncovered in excavations which first started in 1894 and were continued again in 1997.

Opposite ancient Kalavria was the impor-tant Peloponnesian city of Troezen. The remains of much of ancient Troezen survive, and many artefacts have been found here. Kalavria was always dependent upon Troezen until archaic times, when it began to shape its own fate. The presence of Myceneans in the area is clear from the many Mycenean vases that have been found. Troezen took part in the Trojan War and was later conquered by the Dorians.

As such, Kalavria began in the early 7th century to flourish, and this prosperity grew in the middle of that century, when the celebrated Kalaurian League was founded, a religious and political confederation of the seven largest city-states of the era: Athens, Aegina, Nauplia, Epidaurus, Hermione, Prasiai, and Orchomenos.

Above: headless statue of a woman wearing a chiton and a himation, from the acropolis of Troezen, early 4th century BC. Archaeological Museum.

PLAN OF THE TEMPLE OF POSEIDON

1. Temple
2. Building A
3. Building B
4. Building Γ
5. Building Δ
6. Building E
7. Exedra
8. Building Z
9. Building H

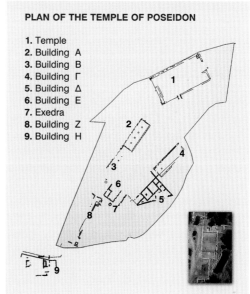

The seat of this League was the Temple of Poseidon, in the centre of the island, and the initial purpose was to hold common functions for the worship of a common god, Poseidon. Immediately, however, this religious alliance expanded in other areas and became a political alliance too. Its aims were to ease trading relations between the member-cities, and to protect the cities in the event of an attack by an enemy which was not part of the alliance. The concept, then, of the European Union, which was born in our era, was applied for the first time by seven city-states of Greece over 2,600 years ago!

Kalavria continued to flourish during the 5th century BC, and the Temple of Poseidon always provided a place of asylum for fugitives. This is where the fanatical anti-Macedonian and great Athenian rhetor Demosthenes sought refuge in 322 BC, when being pursued by the Macedonian soldiers who had taken over the whole of Greece. Once he realised that escape was impossible, he committed suicide by drinking a poison that he had hidden on himself.

Alexander the Great's Macedonians were followed by the Romans. In AD 396, the Goths, led by Alaric, totally destroyed Troezen and Kalavria. There then followed the long Byzantine period, with Frankish (Western) rule coming in 1204, and Turkish occupation in 1460. Until then, Poros had been practically abandoned by its inhabitants because of the many pirate raids.

The new inhabitants who subsequently came to the island first based themselves at Kastelli, near today's Roloi (clock). They were all Arvanites - Orthodox Christians of Albanian origin - from the Peloponnese who were being pursued by the Turks. These new inhabitants, just like the Hydraiots and the Spetsiots, were exceptionally good at commerce and shipping, and gradually became wealthy.

They did not, however, take an active part in the liberation struggle of 1821 as the Turks were based only a few metres from the island. They did, of course, have the support of the Russians, who had already based themselves at a military dockyard on the island. The first Greek dockyard was set up in 1828, and this remained on Poros for many years, eventually being moved to Salamis.

In 1831, an event took place at the dockyard which showed just how destructive civil war can be. The Hydraiots, the Spetsiots and the Psarians, who were opposed to Capodistrias, the first Governor of Greece, attacked the dockyard, with Andreas Miaoulis at their head. They blew up two ships and then left. Thankfully, the Revolution was over, as they would not have dared do such a thing whilst it still continued. Thankfully, the achievements of Miaoulis and his fellow fighters during the Revolution were so great, that they could not be forgotten as a result of this unpleasant event.

1. The first naval dockyards at the port of Poros.
2. The Monument to the Heroes of Troezen, 1912-1922.

YESTERDAY
& TODAY

The fame of ancient Kalavria had been long
forgotten by the time the new inhabitants began
to arrive on the then deserted island in
the 1460s from the Peloponnesian coasts
opposite. They were, as we mentioned above,
Orthodox Christian Arvanites attempting
to flee the persecutions of the Turks, who had
just conquered Greece. There were no Turks
on the island; there was always, however, the
fear of pirates, and for this reason they chose a
rocky hill on which to build a defensive
settlement, and called it Kastelli (castle).
In the beginning, life on the island was difficult,
but not as bad as for their compatriots
who had disembarked on Hydra, persecuted as
well by the Turks. On Poros there was water at
least, and the island was anything but rocky
and barren. They took up farming and animal
husbandry, professions which were the main
occupations of the inhabitants of Poros for many
years. They then gradually turned to commerce
and fishing, following the example of the
Hydraiots and the Spetsiots, who were
progressing day by day. They followed in their
steps, then, and with great success. They
did not make as much money as their
compatriots on the other islands, but they made
enough to become prosperous and for Kastelli
to grow. It spread out over the neighbouring
hill and as far as the sea. Poros shared in
the partial autonomy that Hydra and Spetses
enjoyed.

And just as everything, on the surface at
least, was going well, the moment came for the
great uprising. Supported by their strong fleet,
the Hydraiots and the Spetsiots proclaimed the
Revolution against the Turks. How could the
Poriots do the same, however, when the enemy
was based only a few metres opposite them?
They remained, then, outside of the immediate

action, assisting secretly in any way they could. The leaders of the Revolution often held their meetings in great secrecy at the monastery of the Zoodochos Pigi. And the moment of liberation finally came. Poros had the great honour in 1828 of hosting the first military dockyard of free Greece. It remained here for many years, before being transferred to Salamis.

It was at this same dockyard in 1831 that the opponents of Governor Capodistrias clashed with his supporters and two war ships were burnt. The dispute passed and time diminished the unpleasant event. A few years later the German architect Ziller built the elegant Progymnasium, the Naval Training School where men of the military navy are still trained today, and beautiful mansions began to be constructed in Poros town. The rhythm of life on the island started to quicken, and the first Athenians began to visit the island. Unfortunately, however, the 20th century had

barely begun when the wars started to follow, one after the other. The Balkan Wars of 1912 and 1913, the First World War, the Second World War, German occupation in 1941, the civil war. Life began again in the 1950s. The summer holiday-makers returned to the pretty town in small engine-powered craft, covered with a canopy to protect them from the sun, and they would set down on the beautiful sandy beach of Neorio for a swim. In 1951 the legendary battleship the Averoff was stationed in the waters of Poros. This was the battleship which liberated the Aegean islands of Lemnos, Lesbos and Chios in 1912. It remained there until 1984, when it took part in the events of Nautical Week during the first ten days of July. After this, it was taken to Palaio Faliro in Athens, where it remains until today. In the meantime, the town of Poros was growing. It grew beyond the channel

and extended leftwards to the neighbourhood of Aspros Gatos and to the right towards Askeli, with the wonderful sands and beautiful pine trees. This beach is the fasting developing area. Large hotels are being built at Askeli, and also at Neorio.

For many years now it is not only ships that have gone to Poros, but also ferryboats which can carry cars, so that visitors can enjoy more of the island. For those in a hurry, there are the 'flying dolphin' hovercraft and catamarans, which leave from Zea or the port of Piraeus, reaching Poros an hour later. In just one day, then, the visitor can go to Poros for a swim, and then make the most of the surfaced road which goes around the whole of this green island, visit the Monastery and the temple of Poseidon, ending up at the Poseidon restaurant, which looks over the town of Poros and its famous strait. Poros today

lives to the rhythm of tourist development, which brings it its greatest income.

Little churches appear all over the island as one tours it. The same happens with the little fishing caiques, which leave continuously, in search of a good haul.

The heart of the town is perched on top of a conical hill, which has a two-storey structure with a clock at its peak. This clock, the Roloi, is the trademark of Poros. It has stood here for over 75 years, like a watch-tower over the whole area, offering a fantastic view to those who climb up as far as here. Opposite is Galata, a seaside resort on the Peloponnesian coast, set in luscious-green surroundings. In between Poros and Galata, a narrow strip of sea, only 300 metres wide, plays with the turquoise waters, forming small, picturesque bays. On this hill, which is a veritable natural fortress, the first houses of Poros were built in the 15th century, so as to be protected from pirate raids. The settlement was called Kastelli and its first inhabitants were Orthodox Christian Arvanites, who came here from the Peloponnese to escape persecution from the Turks. Later, the neighbouring hill was inhabited as well, the one which today has a half-ruined mill at its peak. Both hills are located on a rocky islet known since antiquity as Sfairia. This strip of sea gradually came to be filled in with alluvial deposits and Sfairia was finally united with the large neighbouring island of ancient Kalavria to form today's Poros. Part of this other island can be seen from the Roloi, and, in contrast with Sfairia, it is thick with pine trees. What can mainly be seen, however, is the port down below, crowded with large and small boats, some moored and others in motion. Those which transport visitors to the various beaches of the island or to Galata opposite. The wharf where the ferryboats and speedboats that serve the Argosaronic connections dock can also be seen. There is much movement, especially during the summer months.

The liveliness of the port impresses the visitor as soon as he disembarks from the boat. The shops, the cafes, the restaurants, all create a special atmosphere. This atmosphere is added to by the sight of the two- and three-storey houses, some of which are neo-classical in design.

A walk along the pier is most enjoyable. On the left-hand side of the road going in a south-easterly direction, opposite the taxi rank, there is an old,

unrenovated two-storey house. This is the mansion
of Kanelopoulos. The rare iron-work of the balconies
and decoration beneath the eaves of the roof are
worth noticing.

A little distance from this mansion there is a
spacious square - the Kolona - with a marble
monument to the war dead. At the peak of the
monument is perched an eagle, with its wings half-
spread. The houses all around are old, although
there are some new houses among them. After this
square is the **square with the town hall,** with the
characteristic marble fountain. This fountain is tall,
cylindrical, with sculpted decoration. There is a third
square even further to the east, Alexandros Koryzis
Square. Koryzis was a prime minister of Greece,
and his marble bust stands in the centre. Round
about this bust, beneath the umbrellas which
provide protection from the summer sun, there are
tables and cafes. The renovated house on the right
was the mansion of Koryzis, and today it houses the
Archaeological Museum of Poros.

There are some fine exhibits in the museum, from
both the island of Poros, especially the famous
sanctuary of Apollo, as well as from the wider

region, such as from Troezen, which had very close relations with Poros, and from Galata, Methana and Hermione. Among the finds, we can mention the column capitals from the sanctuary of Poseidon, such as the Doric capital dating to the end of the 6h century BC, the 5th-century BC Poros stone capital, and the Ionic Poros stone capital from the sanctuary's stoa dating to the 4th century BC, which are in the ground floor exhibition hall. In the same hall are kept the Vote of Troezen, tomb stelai, Mycenean finds from Troezen, Methana and the Galata region, 6th-century BC inscriptions from Methana, and much more.

The upper hall contains mainly pottery finds. Among the exhibits are the Mycenean finds from Ayios Konstantinos at Methana dating to the 13th century BC, chamber tombs from the Galata region dating to the 14th and 13th century BC, vases from the geometric period from around Troezen and Hermione, and black-figure vases from Troezen dating to the 6th-5th century BC.

Boats are anchored along the whole length of the dock. Among them are small cruise ships, fishing caiques and small craft. The latter transport visitors to the Peloponnesian coast opposite. From this point, those going by foot will follow the uphill path which passes through the famous Lemonodasos, the lemon tree forest, so as to enjoy one of the most wonderful routes. If indeed they have the good fortune to be here in the springtime when the lemon trees are budding, then the pleasure will be even greater. It is said that the aroma from the lemon trees is so strong that, when the wind is blowing, it reaches as far as Poros. There high above, within the forest, with the water running from the watermills, visitors will be able to rest at a taverna, with the satisfaction that they have just covered a wonderful route.

4

5

1. The port with the church of the Evangelistria.
2. The square with the Town Hall.
3. Alexandros Koryzis Square.
4, 5. Exhibits from the Archaeological Museum.

There are lanes leading from the coastal road up to the **Roloi**. These lanes, with the white houses, blue doors and windows and whitewashed steps, are very reminiscent of the architecture of the Aegean islands. One of these lanes, the central one before the peak of the hill, passes by the **Metropolitan church**, a grey, austere and imposing building. From here upwards, the ascent becomes steeper and perhaps more tiring. Yet, as we noted at the beginning of the chapter, we will be compensated by the wonderful view.

The descent can be made from the west slope of the hill. There are pretty lanes with white walls here as well. And there are also whitewashed steps against the background of the blue sea and the beach at **Galata**. Neither are the greenery nor the pretty bougainvillaeas nor the flowerpots absent. As the visitor descends then he will pass through the neighbourhood of Ai-Giorgis. There are many interesting things here. A neo-classical building stands neglected in front of a small square. This is the two-storey mansion of Revegikas. The marble buttresses and the heavy, black iron of the balcony catch the eye. The doors and windows above are closed. On the ground floor there is a supermarket and next to it an expensive shop. Further down, at the end of the road, is something rather different. The one-storey, neo-classical **shop of Grivas** proudly stands refurbished, reminiscent of past times. Its old doors with the wonderful design, painted in the original dark olive-green colour, the white frames which surround them, its walls painted in an open yellow, have literally resurrected it. Yet, even inside it appears as though nothing has changed from the time when its owner built it and worked on it with much love, primarily as a textiles shop.

All the wood furnishings are still there, the wooden shelves, the cupboards with their drawers and the goods arranged as then. Even the elegant white enamel labels, with their firm black letters which identified the goods are still there. The efforts of a lifetime do not then appear to have disappeared within the century or so that has passed since then.

1

2

The docks at Poros are circular at the point where the ferryboats moor. From the coastal road at a little distance from the pier, one can see the house of Capodistrias, the first Governor of Greece after the Revolution of 1821, behind the empty space in between two neo-classical buildings. Nearby, the **mansion of Deimezis** stands tall on a rock nearby. With its white garden fence, dark grey stone, and white door and window frames, it looks like a typical Hydraiot house.

The coastal road turns, continuing towards the north-east in a straight line. Several old cannons are set up at the docks, and some heavy anchors from an old war ship have also been set up. They are in the position where the first Greek dockyards were. A little further down to the left, in between the sea and the road, is the large neo-classical building designed by the celebrated German architect Ziller. This building is commonly known as the **Progymnastria** and houses the military navy training school. Despite its great size, the building looks especially elegant, with its white windows and white eaves. Nearby is a crossing with a road going to the right. This road circles around Sfairia, going back down to the port again. Thanks to this road, the visitor can enjoy a view of the Poros strait and see the islet of **Bourtzi** from close up. This islet lies at the south-east entrance of the strait and has a fortress wall built upon it.

The central road ends at the neck which unites Sfairia with Kalavria. A small canal, known as the **Kanali**, has been opened up here, over which passes a bridge. From here, the road divides into two main directions which follow the coasts, to the left towards Neoria and to the right towards Askeli, the Monastery of the Zoodochos Pigi, and the sanctuary of Poseidon. There is also a third road which travels into the hinterland of the island through a pine forest. It goes round in a circle, passing the sanctuary of Poseidon, to eventually meet the second road near Monastiri.

1. The Kanali.
2. The Progymnasium, a work by Ziller.

Mikro and Megalo Neorio

After the Kanali, the road to the right passes through the village of Aspros Gatos, following the coast, which is full of small boats. The picture of these colourful boats, with the Progymnastirio and the hill with the town of Poros in the background is delightful.

To the west, an old red villa with white plaster railings on its balcony and verandas, looks over the strait of Poros from high up. It is thick with tall pine trees all around it. This is the villa **Galini**, which means 'peacefulness' in Greek, perhaps the most beautiful house in Poros, which once hosted Arthur Miller and George Seferis, the Greek poet and Nobel Prize winner.

The route has a pleasant surprise in store, and this is the first view of the beautiful sandy beach of **Mikro Neorio**. This is a small, organised beach with a thick pine forest next to it.
A short distance from this beach, after the turn in the road, there is another beach, much larger than the first, which forms an open butterfly pattern. This is **Megalo Neorio**. The beautiful sands here are also surrounded by thick, verdant pine trees. There is, however, something more: the water sports facilities.

The next surprise is even greater, as the road approaches the magical **little harbour of Agapi,** with its little sandy beach, crystal-clear waters and the pine trees which literally hang over it. This is perhaps the most picturesque beach in the whole of Poros.

The journey on the road which follows the coast continues. On the next bay there are the remains of the storehouses of the Russian naval yard. Opposite this is the charming little island of **Daskalio,** with the church of the Panayia and only a few, although tall, pine trees. The road - now a dirt road - passes over the most westerly point of the island, with the beautiful cove and rocky island of Petra, continuing in a circle within a thick pine forest, connecting with the surfaced road a little before the sanctuary of Poseidon.

important sites of worship in ancient Greece which began to operate in the late Geometric period, and which later also developed into a political centre when the League of Kalaureia (as the island was then known) was founded in the 7th century. This was the first time in history when the seven largest city-states of ancient Greece (Athens, Aegina, Epidaurus, Hermione, Prasiai, Nauplion and Orchomenos) set up an alliance which had as its centre the temple of Poseidon Kalavreios. An alliance which could be compared - and why not? - with today's European Union, created after 2,500 and more years. The excavations at the site first began in 1894 by the Swedish archaeologists S. Wide and L. Kjellberg, to be resumed again in 1997 by the Swedish Institute at Athens. The ruins of the foundations of the temple of Poseidon are in the north-west side of the site. The

Sanctuary of Poseidon - Vagionia

After Kanali, the road continues in a northerly direction, passing through a relatively new neighbourhood of Poros, and soon enters a thick pine forest.

The road leads further into the hinterland of the island, ascending the hill of Profitis Ilias with many curves. After about 2 kilometres, a road to the right soon leads to the Poseidonio bar-cafe, built high up in an advantageous position with a wonderful view over the town of Poros and the strait, both during the day and at night.

The central road continues its upward climb, finally reaching a plateau with a view over a valley which spreads out to the left and descends as far as the sea. This is **Fousa,** well-known from ancient times for its wine. The sanctuary of Poseidon will soon also make its appearance. This was one of the most

temple was built in the Doric order in the 6th century BC, with six columns on its narrow sides and 12 along its long sides. There is at least one column capital from the temple in the Archaeological Museum in Poros town, in which other column capitals from the sanctuary are also exhibited. Seven auxiliary buildings have been found near the temple, most of which are stoas or vestibules. A plan of the site set up at the entrance shows the auxiliary buildings labelled A through to G. This plan notes that the excavations on building D were conducted recently (1999 and 2000). It is quite difficult to study the site, however, as most of the porous limestone pieces from the ruins were removed to Hydra in order to build the old Hydraiot houses!

1. The temple of Poseidon.
2. The islet of Daskaleio.
3. The little port at Agapi.

1

The area around the sanctuary, with a view over the Saronic Gulf is quite beautiful and some people have gone so far as to build an isolated villa on the slope of some hill, their only communication with the outside world being a dirt road.

The only exception is the road which begins near the temple and continues down to the pretty bay of Vagionia with the settlement of the same name. The route through the luscious-green gorge which terminates at a bay which is closed off on both sides by steep cliffs. The pebbly beach here is beautiful, with crystal-clear waters, forming a large butterfly pattern, which has a little taverna at its centre. Further inwards, there are several cypress trees, pines and olive groves with, at the edge of the bay, clambering up the steep slope of a hill, some... privileged houses. The view from up there is splendid, the landscape idyllic. When enjoying this wonderful landscape, it is difficult for one to imagine, if one does not already know, that below the peaceful waters of the bay lies a sunken ancient city. This was the second largest ancient city after Kalavria. Whenever the waters are calm, the roads and ruins of the houses can be seen on the bed of the sea.

1. The beach at Askeli.
2. The beach of Vagionia.

2

Askeli - Zoodochos Pigi Monastery

Askeli is one of the most beautiful beaches not just of Poros, but of the whole of the Argosaronic. The clean and clear waters, the wonderful sands and the fantastic thick green vegetation which surrounds it all contributed to its speedy development as a tourist resort. The hotels, bars, restaurants and water sports facilities ensure the visitor a comfortable stay. The distance from the port of Poros, with which there are regular bus connections, is only 3 kilometres. The road taken by the bus is that which turns right after the Kanali, to follow the coast.

The bus continues further east, reaching the **Monastery of the Zoodochos Pigi of Kalavria** after another kilometre. A stream bursting with vegetation runs abruptly into the sea. The beautiful monastery, with its white walls on all sides and the church in the centre, is built on the side of the stream. A little before the monastery, on the left of the road, the little church of the Ayii Anargyri welcomes visitors. A small cafe

next to it, its little tables below the plane trees, is just what is needed to provide all those who have come here by foot with a rest.

The monastery was built in the 18th century next to a spring (pigi in Greek), the water of which was said to have therapeutic powers. The monastery was thus dedicated to the Panayia Zoodochos Pigi, the Virgin Mary Life-Giving Source, and it celebrates its feast day on the Friday after Easter, with one of the island's largest festivals. From high up, the wings of the monastery with the monks' cells can be seen extending at both sides. They are two-storey and their roofs are covered in red tiles. The walls are tall and fortress-like, in order to protect from pirates.

The church is built in the centre of the forecourt, on the site of an older and smaller church. It is in the basilica-style with an octagonal dome and a tall belfry over its entrance. There are no wall-paintings inside, but it does contain important icons and a wonderful wood-carved iconostasis, which, as tradition has it, was built in Cappodocia in Asia Minor.

The monastery played an important role during the War of Independence, as it was a meeting place for many of the leading figures. Indeed, the Hydraiot admiral Andreas Miaoulis and the Tobazis family, fighters in the War of 1821, are buried here. The monastery played a similar role during World War II, when it was a hideout for members of the resistance.

A footpath at the eastern exit of the monastery leads down to the beach. Before going down this path, it is worth stopping for a while to enjoy the view from the small, paved forecourt. The stream with the pine and olive trees leads sharply down to the sea. A patch of sand and a few little tavernas can be seen on the beach. Opposite is the luscious-green coast of the Peloponnese, with the azure sea and the strait of Poros in between.

The visitor can of course also go down to the beach by car, from the road a little before the monastery. Yet, it is only a short distance away, about 15 minutes by foot, and the walk along the footpath is definitely worth it. If you are lucky enough to be here in the summer, then you will be able to enjoy a swim in the crystal-clear waters and a meal in one of the tavernas on the beach.

The sea will shine beneath the rays of the sun.
A surfer will be crossing the open sea and the light
wind blowing through the strait of Poros will fill his
sail of many colours.

We do not believe that the traveller could ask for
anything more during his or her stay in Poros.

1, 2, 4. *Views from the internal and external decoration*
   of the monastery of the Zoodochos Pigi.
3. *The beach beneath the monastery.*

HYDRA

The Noble Lady of the Argosaronic

Hydra's fame has spread beyond the borders of Greece, reaching as far as the other side of the world. All visitors to the island talk of the pretty harbour with the traditional houses built spread over the rocky slopes of the surrounding hills. Of the wonderful mansions built in grey stone with a white outline around the windows, the mansions built by the Hydraiot captains with much love, when their merchant fleet ruled the whole of the Mediterranean and brought great wealth to the island. In the days when little Hydra flourished and was indeed the noble lady of the Argosaronic.

This economic prosperity was to be cut off by the Greek Revolution of 1821 against the Turks. The Hydraiots, who loved freedom more than wealth and grandeur, threw themselves into the Struggle with a passion. They transformed their commercial ships into battleships, arming them with cannons, and, along with the Spetsiots and Psarians, successfully fought the Turkish fleet. At the head of the Greek fleet, the idol of the Hydraiots until today even, was their compatriot Andreas Miaoulis.

The war lasted for seven whole years, and the miracle came in the end. Greece had managed to defeat a whole empire and free itself. Little Hydra and its ships had played a decisive role in this struggle.

The price of victory was, however, ultimately very heavy for the Hydraiots. They had used up all their wealth for the Struggle, and most of their ships had been destroyed. It seemed that the game was finally up, and the Hydraiots began to abandon their barren island. Then there was another miracle, and this time without a war, without a fleet and without cannons. In the 1950s, artists and intellectuals from Greece and abroad began to congregate on the island and immortalise its charms with their pens and with their paint brushes. The intellectuals were followed by the tourists, whose number was constantly on the rise. Within a few years, the island had evolved into an intellectual and artistic centre and Hydra again became the noble lady of the Argosaronic.

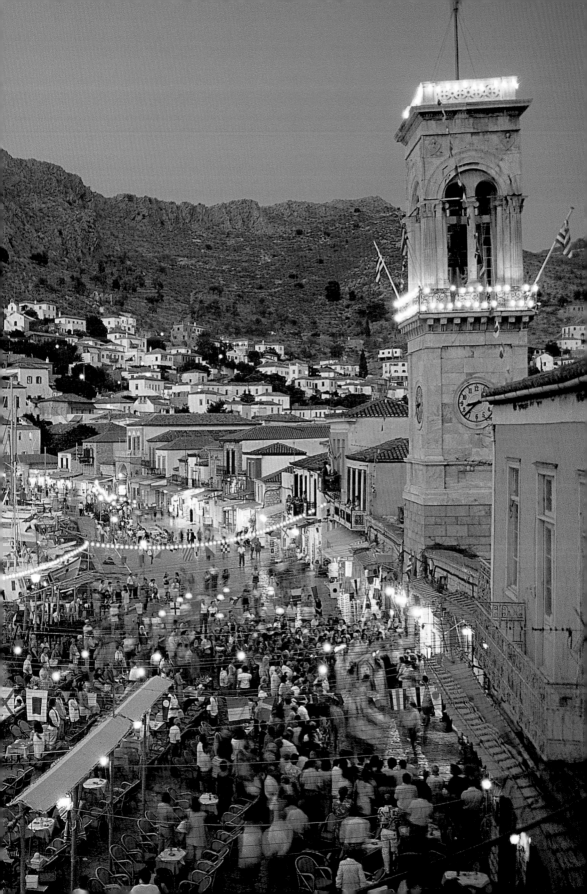

Geography

Hydra is located between the Saronic and the Argolic Gulfs, at a distance of four to five miles from the Peloponnesian coast. It is long and narrow, with a length of around 20 kilometres and a broadest width of 4 km. It has a surface area of 50 kilometres and a coastline of 55 km.

The island has less than 3000 permanent residents, in contrast with the summer months, when this figure increases greatly. There are daily connections with Piraeus, which is 37 nautical miles away.

Morphology

In contrast with many of the Argosaronic islands, Hydra is for the most part bare and rocky with pine trees only in its south-west section. The highest mountain, Eros (590 m.) is in the centre of the island, to the south of Hydra town.

There are a few small bays in its northern coasts, such as Mantraki, the port of Hydra, and Ayios Georgios at Bisti. There are two larger bays in the southern coast, Ayios Nikolaos and Limnionizas. As for the valleys, the main one is that at Episkopi in the southern part of the island.

IS. KAM

IS. VLIHOS

VI

IS. PALAMIDA

IS. KIVOTOS
IS. KALES   IS. PANAGIA   KIMOMENI
IS. ERIMONISI

IS. DOKOS

Molos

MT. PETROKORIFI   MT. KORIFI

IS. PETASI

MT. ZOGIERI

+ 188

+ 290

MT. FARDI SPITHARI   NISITSA

MT. TSAKONI

MT. GERAKINA   Episkopi

IS. PONDIKONISI

+ 348

Agios Georgios

Agios Nikolaos   + 236   BARBARI   CAPE AGIOU IOANOU

CAPE BISTI   VIGLA   BISTI

IS. TSIGKRI
IS. ERIMONISIA

The islet of Dokos

This islet, lying in between Hydra and the Peloponnesian coast, was for the Hydraiots the main source of the beautiful grey stone with which they built most of their houses and mansions. There was a quarry in operation here many years ago in order to mine the stone. The islet, which is bare and rocky on its southern side, has a surface area of 12 square kilometres.

N

CAPE MPETISTA

CAPE MANIATI

CAPE KASTEVAS

MEGALI VIGLA

CAPE ZOURVAS

ALONAKI

KATEHOS

M. Theotokou Zourva

KOUKOU
+ 290

ZOURVA
+ 259

AGIA PARASKEVI

⚓ IDRA Mandraki

M. Agias Triados

M. Agiou Nikolaou

MT. OMPORI
+ 506   + 519

M. Agias Matronis

MT. MALIES

LIMNIONIZA
+ 464

CAPE MAVRO MATI

M. Profiti Ilia

MT. KONTARIA

CAPE TSIGARI

MT. PIRGOS
+ 557

Agios Petros

KLIMAKI

gii Taxiarhes   Panagia

Hristos

Agios Nikolaos

CAPE RIGAS

OKA

LEGEND

▦	Surfaced road
—	Non-surfaced road
⊤	Archaeological site
⚲	Church
⌂	Monastery
▨	Castle
⛱	Beach
⋀	Camp site

MYTHOLOGY & HISTORY

In ancient times the island was known as Hydrea. This is how the great ancient historians Hecataeus and Herodotus referred to it. Heysichius of Alexandria was the first to call it 'Hydra' in his Lexicon. The Venetians called the island Sidra, and only in 1768 is it again referred to as Hydra, by Lozie in his 'History of the Venetian Republic.'

Hydra was occupied in the Mycenean period. This is apparent from the excavations conducted to the south-west of the town, in the region of Vlychos. Any earlier periods of occupation would have been for a short duration and took place when the island was used as a way station between the Peloponnese and the Cyclades. The Dryopes appear to have been the first race to pass through Hydra and settle here permanently. They were a mountain people who lived around the mountains of Oitis and Parnassos, and who were later displaced by the Dorians. The Dryopes were able, more than any other peoples, to face the difficult conditions on the island and partake, as in their original homeland, in animal husbandry.

Around two or so centuries after the arrival of the Dryopes, dated to the 13th century BC, the Dorians descended, marking thus the end of the Mycenean period on Hydra.

In his reference to Hydrea, Herodotus writes that in the 6th century BC fugitives from Samos who had unsuccessfully attempted to overthrow the tyrant Polykrates, were sailing around on the Aegean and disembarked at Siphnos, the island that was rich in gold mines. Here, they violently grabbed 100 talents and, with this money, purchased Hydra from the inhabitants of Hermione on the Peloponnese opposite, to whom the island then belonged. The Samians later sold Hydra to the Troezens, the inhabitants of the then powerful city to the north, opposite Poros, under whose control it remained until the 4th century BC.

We do not have any information on the island for the classical period, aside from a reference by the historian and geographer Stephanus Byzantius, who mentions that there was a shepherd named Evagis on the island who was also a comic playwright. Only a few details survive for the periods of Macedonian and Roman rule and for the long Byzantine period. This fact has led to the conviction that Hydra was unoccupied during these years, something which is not completely accurate. The truth is that the constant pirate raids forced a large number of the population to abandon the island, whilst the rest distanced themselves from the coasts and dispersed around the hinterland. We are led to this

View of the town of Hydra, 1795, Thomas Hope.

conclusion by the fact that many bronze and gold Byzantine coins have been found at the Bishopric, as well as evidence for occupation during much earlier periods. The Byzantine period on the island ended in 1204 with the coming of Venetian rule. The subsequent war between the Venetians and the Turks led to the island coming under Turkish rule, although this did not result in any changes to the demographic problem. The obscurity and apparent desertion of Hydra was ended in around 1470 by the Arvanites Orthodox Christians who passed over to the island from the Peloponnese to escape Turkish persecution. These Arvanites were the descendants of those whom the Despots of Mystra, Kantakouzenos and Palaiologos had invited to settle in their region, in order to increase the falling population of the Peloponnese. The new settlers on Hydra merged with the old, and together they began anew to build the first

houses of the town on the hill of Kiafas, and to throw themselves into the struggle for survival.
The dry and barren land of the island forced them to turn to the sea. The beginning was made with the building of small ships, for them to proceed a little later - in the mid-18th century - to building larger ones. Shortly before the end of the 18th century, they Hydraiots had 150 large merchant ships in their possession. It was clear that with such a fleet, Hydra could achieve much in the fields of commerce and shipping, as indeed happened. The island was of course helped in this direction by other events and coincidences

As for relations with ruling Turkey, Hydra enjoyed quite a few privileges. The island was governed by local Hydraiot notables and a Turkish representative, who was appointed by the Hydraiots themselves. Two wars took place during the period of Turkish

rule which were exceptionally favourable to the Hydraiots. The first was the war between Russia and Turkey (1768-1774), which ended with Turkey's defeat and the signing of the Treaty of Kutchuk Kaynarca, by which the Bosphorus strait was opened, meaning that Hydraiot ships could now sail through to the Black Sea and supply the Mediterranean with wheat. The second war was that against Napoleon during which the British blockaded the Mediterranean. The courageous Hydraiots, however, were brave enough to break through the blockade and thus control all shipping through the Mediterranean. This was when Ibrahim Pasha, the Ottoman Commander-in-Chief, described Hydra as a 'Little England.'

These excellent captains would unload their goods in the west and return loaded with luxurious furniture, porcelains and paintings from Italy and France and, of course, with lots of money, so that Hydra became the wealthiest region of Greece. The large mansions in grey stone were built under the supervision of Italian craftsmen and were furnished according to western prototypes. Naturally, this wealth also led to social progress and many functions and balls were organised in special halls, at which foreign orchestras performed.

The captains and the people of Hydra may have loved all this luxury and wealth. Yet, there was something which for them had even more significance: their love of freedom. The hour for the uprising against the Turks had arrived. The Peloponnesian opposite had already risen, and now they were inviting the Hydraiots, who had power, to help them. The notables at first hesitated, but the people were not to be restrained. They revoked the Turkish representative and appointed Antonios Oikonomos to be their own governor. The notables agreed to this and Hydra finally took its part in the Revolution of 1821. Yet, the island was not alone. Alongside it were another two islands which contributed their fleets to the Struggle: neighbouring Spetses and distant Psara. The leader of the collective fleet was the Hydraiot Admiral Andreas Miaoulis. Next to him were brave fighters, such as Voulgaris, Tobazis, Sachtouris, Tsamados, etc. Their achievements became known throughout the whole of Europe.

The merchant ships, which were armed and converted into battle ships, brought fear to the Turks. Their fireships - small ships loaded with explosives,

The statue of Andreas Miaoulis.

which slid around in the dark and even dared to enter the Turkish ports and blow up the battle ships - became legendary.

The Struggle lasted for a whole seven years, and in the end the Greeks won and Greece was liberated. Hydra and the other two islands were among the major contributors to this victory. Yet, the Hydraiots had given their all: their ships, money and barren land could no longer support them. In the mid-19th century they were forced to turn to sponge diving, which unfortunately declined after a few years, along with the island. Most of the sailors gradually began to abandon the island, and it took a great painter, Hadjikyriakos Gikas, to appear on the island in the 1950s, and for many films with internationally-renowned stars to be made here, for the island to begin to live again and finally to become an international tourist centre. Perhaps one of the greatest presences on the island during that heyday was the great Canadian singer-songwriter Leonard Cohen, who wrote some of his finest tunes here.

YESTERDAY & TODAY

Architecture: Life was difficult for those first settlers on the island. They were Arvanites, Orthodox
Christians of Albanian descent, who came to the Peloponnese in the 15th century to escape persecution
from the Turks. They were aware of what they would
have to face on this dry and barren land, but they
chose to try their luck, just as long as they could live
free. They have been called unsubdued, frugal, hard-
ened, stubborn. All these characterisations are cor-
rect. The same holds true for the Greeks who came
after them from various parts of Greece. They were
also being persecuted by the Turks and had to coex-
ist with these first settlers in order to face the difficul-
ties together. And that is what happened. In the beginning, they threw themselves into animal husbandry
and agriculture. Yet, they quickly realised that, isolated as they were, their only opportunity was the sea.

Their first houses were nothing more than wooden
huts and their first ships simple wooden hulls. Slowly,
slowly, they began to use stone, whilst some, who had
come from the slave galleys of Egypt taught them the
craft of shipbuilding using wood, and they began to
build real ships. The first stone houses appeared at
Kiafa, the rocky hill to the south of the port, with its
steep slopes, its surrounding streams providing safe-
ty. With these, they created a defensive settlement,
with tall walls, narrow lanes and covered walkways.
This kind of architecture was a combination of the
styles found on the Aegean islands and on the mainland. Unfortunately, the whole of the settlement was
destroyed, and only three of its churches remain
today. The Hydraiots rebuilt their settlement though,
preserving many of the elements of the old, whilst also
gradually expanding their town towards the port, and
a little later, towards today's Kaminia and Vlycho.

The materials they used were stone and wood,
which they acquired primarily from the neighbouring
islet of Dokos. In order to build with stone, they used
a mortar made from clay, known as 'kokkina,' to
which they later added straw and limestone. For the
mansions, this mortar was called 'koursani' and was
enriched with sand, ground tiles, and an earth
known as 'pitreliana.' Wood was used to 'bind' the
ordinary houses, whilst in the mansions they used
iron. Wood was, however, necessary in both types of
houses for the construction of the roof, the 'liakos,'
as they called it. For this, they used the trunks of
mainly cypress trees, laying them out side-by-side a
little apart one from the other. Over the trunks they
added a layer of thin branches of planks, seaweed,
'kokkina,' a layer of earth around 30 cm. thick, and a
layer of earth mixed with clay and limestone. On top
of all this they placed the tiles. The final layer was of
mortar, so as to ensure dryness. The 'liakos' was
later covered with ceramic tiles, and few houses
today still have their original structure.

The earliest houses consisted of just one
orthogonal room, and the auxiliary areas were
detached, just as happens in farmhouses today.
This house design evolved by adding other rooms
on one or more floors. These rooms were adjoining
and had the same arrangement. The larger houses
were built in the shape of an L or had wings on both
sides. The exterior was simple. There was one
external stone staircase, and usually a wooden
staircase inside. The interior of the house was
divided into the 'andres' (men's) or 'good salon,' the

bedrooms, kitchen, oven, storeroom and bathroom. There was a yard with tall walls, quite a bit of vegetation, and the essential cistern for water storage. In some cases, there is a shop on the ground floor or a lounge and kitchen. For the facade, the white of the limestone initially predominated. Later, they began to use ochra or even stronger colours. The same happened with the door and window frames, which were at first painted in a light grey or green, and later in far more vibrant colours.

As for the mansions, these kept many of the features of the ordinary houses. That which made them stand apart, however, was the size and luxury of the interior. Indeed, most of these mansions had been built by Italian artisans who had been invited over for this purpose. Another characteristic is the white outline around the windows, which breaks up the monotone grey of the building.

Inside, the mansions are roomy with tall ceilings. In addition to the standard rooms, there was often a room in which to smoke a narghile (a water-pipe), and a smaller room with an icon stand. The luxurious furniture, brought over from west and east, is impressive.

All this wealth, which had accumulated on the

island by the early 19th century, was the product of a collective effort on the part of the Hydraiot captains and their men. With their courage and strengths they succeeded in making their merchant fleet rule the Mediterranean waves, even breaking through the blockade imposed by the British. A story which is told of an unexpected meeting between the then young Andreas Miaoulis, future admiral of the Greek fleet, with the British admiral Nelson is revealing. Miaoulis had been arrested for infringing the British blockade, an act punishable by death. The British admiral, full of curiosity, asked to see this brave young man. When Nelson saw Miaoulis standing bravely before him, he asked him "What would you do if you were in my position?" To which Miaoulis, undaunted, answered, "I would hang you." At which Nelson did not simply allow him to live, but he freed him.

Customs & traditions - Traditional dress:

The Hydraiots may have lived through tumultuous times. A tough struggle for survival when they first settled on the island, later struggles on the sea and at war. Yet, this did not prevent them from expressing their religious faith at every opportunity and from preserving their local customs. The 150 churches and monasteries on Hydra, an island with a relatively small population, demonstrate the islanders' religious faith. As for the local customs, many of these are fading or have disappeared altogether. There are, however, some which are maintained until our days. The most important of these is the wedding. In the old days, the Hydraiot wedding included features which we do not encounter on any other islands. We will not go into details about the 'making of the bed,' which continues to take place throughout the whole of Greece. This is when guests and relatives offer their gifts to the couple-to-be by placing them on the bridal bed. We should, however, mention the 'washing of the bride's hair,' which is done on the Saturday, the day before the wedding, by two married women who themselves have successful marriages. These same women must 'brush the bride's hair' on the Sunday morning before the wedding.Also characteristic is the gesture by the father of the bride towards his daughter at the door of the house, when he gives her a pouch containing gold coins or jewellery before the whole family leaves for the church. The bride would wear the traditional formal wedding dress, on which stood out the 'kontogouni' (a short pelisse) made of silk velvet with gold embroidery which they called the 'yianniotiko,' and the 'tseperi,' an embroidered headscarf which was also made of silk. The tsemperi meant that the women could not wear a necklace, but they wore instead a gold pin, the 'lalana,' over their breast. The bride and the groom would meet in the church. If the groom was a notable, then once the service was completed he would remove the tsemperi from the bride, and replace it with a fez with a golden tassel and kiss her. The wedding banquet was held at lunch-time, whilst the celebration for friends took place in the evening, with much song and dance to the accompaniment of local instruments which then, as now, were the violin and the lute.

The New Year's customs on Hydra are of especial interest. The doors of the house remain open from the morning, as the head of the household awaits the first visitor who will pass over the threshold uninvited. He will then hang a gift around the visitor's neck with a lace and they will have lunch together. If the head of the household just happens to be a notable, then the lucky visitor will surely receive the gift of a gold florin.

The custom which most surprises, however, is that of the Epitaphios, the Good Friday funeral procession of Christ, at Kamini. At this village, the Epitaphios proceeds into the sea, in an invocation to Christ to keep the waters calm and so help the sailors. The common custom of the burning of the effigy of Judas takes place on the night of the Resurrection.

Events: The following festivals take place on Hydra: on 20 August at the Monastery of the Profitis Ilias, on 25 July at the Monastery of Ayia Evpraxia, on 25 March at the Monastery by the port, and on 14 November at Ayios Konstantinos the Hydraiot at Kiafa.

The Miaoulia festival takes place on the nearest weekend to 21 June each year in honour of the Hydraiot Admiral and hero of the Revolution of 1821 Andreas Miaoulis. It lasts for three days, and includes boat races, swimming competitions, dance, etc. On the last day there is a reconstruction of the firing of the Turkish flagship with Bengal lights, and food and drink are on offer.

1. Despite the expansion of technology today, the elderly small traders of the island insist upon traditional methods of transport.
2. Traditional women's dress of Hydra.

Local cuisine: Since we are talking about food, let's say a couple of words about the local cuisine. The almonds of Hydra are widely celebrated, as are the pears served with a coloured bow and cloves. The sugar-baklava is another popular desert of a thin-layered pastry with walnuts and syrup. As for the food, we note the pasta and myzithra (a soft cheese) dish, and the 'boubari' (stomach filled with rice, mince and spices and baked in the oven).

Arts and letters: The Hydra of yesterday was the island of the captains, the heroes and the politicians. This little island has given Greece five prime ministers and around fifty government ministers. Today it is the island of the people of the arts and letters. Yet, the roots of these people are, of course, located in yesterday, when great figures, such as the historian Georgios Kriazis, Andreas Miaoulis, the historian, folklorist and member of the Athens Academy A. Lignos, the historian and folklorist A. Manikis, the professors of ophthalmology Spilios Haramis and I. Haramis, and many others lived.

And yet today, the list of Hydraiot intellectuals and artists who, along with their distinguished colleagues, lived and live on the island is still long. Among them, and including those who are still resident on Hydra for at least some of the year, we find great painters, writers, academics and Nobel prize winners: Hadjikyriakos Gikas, Vyzantios, George Seferis, Odysseus Elytis, Petsalis, Pikionis, Henry Miller, Patrick Leigh Fermor and, last but not least, Leonard Cohen.

2

THE PORT OF HYDRA

The traveller visiting the Argosaronic for the first time is impatient to glimpse a sight of the celebrated Hydra. Yet, as the boat begins to approach the bare island, not much of a great impression is at first made. But suddenly, just before entering the port, something miraculous happens! All that the visitor has seen and heard up until this point pales into insignificance in front of the reality. A closed bay, with rocky hills all around it and mountains behind, stands before him. The town is built spread out on all sides over the rocks, a town the like of which he has never seen before. Two- and three-storey houses, all built in grey stone, following an austere, frugal design. They look like giant cubes with tiles or a roof for the lid. There is almost no external decoration, the only exception being the white cornice around the door and window frames, which somewhat dissipates the monotony of the grey. Some of the houses stand out because of their size: these are the famed mansions of the captains, decorating the town. All around the quay are countless colourful boats, small and large, which add their own note to this magical picture.

Before entering the port, the boat turns before the east cannon station which, as with the one in the west opposite, protected the entrance to the port

during the years of the War of Independence against the Turkish yoke. There, within a raised square, is a bronze statue of the Hydraiot admiral and leader of the Struggle Andreas Miaoulis, who, despite the years which have passed, remains the idol of the Hydraiots. The admiral wears his military naval outfit and holds onto the wheel of a battle ship. The road beneath the square leads to the organised beach of Mantraki.

From here the visitor who wishes to go for a walk along the port of Hydra will encounter, whilst strolling along the length of the waterfront in the direction of the town centre, two large, identical buildings, the second of which is home to the port authority. The beautiful, two-storey building a little further down is the **Historical Archive and Museum** of Hydra. Amongst the Archives are important documents

The Historical Archive and Museum of Hydra.

which highlight Hydra's leading role, especially in the 18th and 19th century, whilst the Museum has exhibits of relics from the Balkan Wars, the First and Second World Wars, a wonderful picture gallery, the arms of Hydraiot Independence fighters, and much more, bringing the whole of the island's heroic past to life within its walls. The Library holds 5,500 volumes, mainly of old editions.

A few metres past the Historical Archive to the left are some three-storey mansions, including the mansion of Tsamados. A little to the south, at the entrance to the middle of the port area and opposite the breakwater is the dock at which the boats and the speedboats moor. There is a lot of movement at this point, as might be expected, and the tables belonging to the row of cafes here are always full. In the south-east corner of the port the 'sea taxis,' as they are called, are always ready to take travellers to the other coasts of the island. These are small speedboats, adapted in such a way so as to be able to travel even when there is a strong meltemi wind. All these boats have a couple of little flags at their sides: the Greek flag and the flag that was used on the island during the War of Independence, with the cross and the slogan "Eleftheria i Thanatos" (freedom or death). This flag does not appear just on the sea taxis, but also on the public buildings. Over 175 years have passed since the Revolution, but it appears that the Hydraiots, just like the Spetsiots, want to keep these memories alive.

From the 'taxi' corner, the waterfront turns to the west. This is the most central section, with

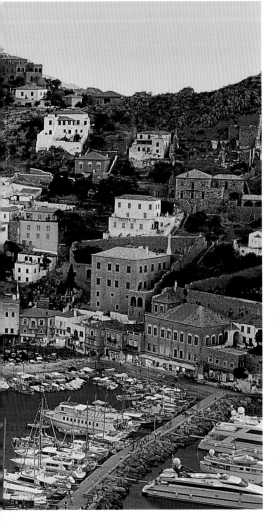

banks, shops, restaurants and cafes. There are quite a lot of people here, especially at nights, that the lights create a phantasmagoric atmosphere. Some people are taking a stroll, whilst others are sitting at the tables. The Monastiri, as the Metropolitan church of Hydra is called, is located somewhere in the middle of the coastal road. It was built in the mid-17th century as the cathedral church of a monastery. It is a three-aisled domed basilica, the aisles of which are separated by rows of columns. The central aisle is dedicated to the **Dormition of the Virgin,** and the church celebrates its feast day on 15 August. The decoration in its interior is rich. The two marble belfries, one of which also has a clock, are impressive. Amongst the graves in the forecourt of the church is that of **Lazaros Kountouriotis**, a patron of the War of 1821, whilst an Ecclesiastical Museum has been opened up in a special hall developed in the section of the monks' cells around the monastery.

The coastal road becomes quite wide at the point in front of the Metropolitan church, creating a three-cornered square. This is the square of Pavlos Kountouriotis, and a grand marble statue of him stands in its centre. From this point on, the waterfront curves northwards. A pier to the right, jutting out like a tongue into the harbour, has all the coloured boats gathered around it. A little road going upwards to the left, all stairs, leads to Tobazis' mansion, now the property of the School of Fine Arts of the Polytechnic University of Athens. Behind its elegant outer door is a veranda with arches, and the view over the sea from here is fantastic.
An even better view can be had from the steep hill with the little church of Ayios Athanasios, from where you can marvel at the whole of the town of Hydra and the surrounding area.

In order to continue the tour of the island, the visitor must return to the coastal road and proceed towards the port exit. To the left, a little before the breakwater, yet another mansion, that of Oikonomos, stands tall.

Periptero - Avlaki - Kaminia

Past the breakwater, the road begins to climb uphill, continuing alongside a rocky road. The first cafeteria which we encounter is built upon the rocks above the crystal-clear blue sea. Its tables are laid out in front. A few metres further up and the road leads to what is perhaps the most beautiful spot on Hydra, the **Periptero**. This is where the west cannon station is located, and below is the famous **Spilia**, or cave, where all the cosmopolitan youth, and not only, gather for their swim. There are a few pine trees on a wide stretch of the road, at the edge of which is a stone wall which starts at the base of the rocks and comes upwards, creating a parapet. At every five metres along the parapet a heavy cannon is pointed towards the sea. These are the same cannons, in the same positions, which protected the port during the years of the Revolution. Below on the rocks, there is a cave in the sea and a rocky islet a little further beyond. Many people gather on the rocks here to enjoy the warm sun, whilst others swim in the sea, enjoying the crystal-clear waters. The parapet proceeds even further along, and along with it the cannons. Now there is another cafeteria, larger than the first. The tables here are situated in among the cannons, whilst a canopy hangs overhead to protect the customers from the sun. A staircase leads down to the rocks, where people are sunbathing and swimming. The sea water at this point takes on an unbelievable colour. A blue indigo, mixed in the shallower areas with emerald and green.

To the left of the road there is a small pine tree forest, in the midst of which stands the beautiful mansion of **Pavlos Kountouriotis**. Behind it is the tall rocky hill of the Myli, with a row of ruined old mills. The last mill, at the peak, is at the same height as the church of Ayios Athanasios on the hill further to the south. The view from up here is sensational, but the footpath is even more steep than that leading up to Ayios Athanasios. From Periptero, the road continues towards the pretty neighbourhood of **Avlaki**, built on a steep slope of this hill and looking over the sea to the Peloponnesian coast opposite from high above. Amongst the houses here, surrounded by pine and cypress trees, is the mansion of Kountouris, an old building with a slate roof and no tiles. It stands at the edge of this neighbourhood, in front of a small cliff with rocks and earth.

After Avlaki, the road continues towards the **Kaminia** (Mikro Kamini and Megalo Kamini), the most charming corner on the whole of Hydra. This is a little harbour with dark brown sands located in among two small, rocky hills. The hills are full of old and new houses, and among them are two tavernas on the two edges of the beach. The first taverna is built at a slight rise, and the other has a yellow and red wall in front of the mole, at which the 'sea taxis' and other small craft dock. The harbour is surrounded by two little breakwaters. Many little boats are moored in behind the breakwaters and in front of the beach, whilst some have even been dragged up onto the sands. All these features together compose a wonderful picture, which is surely an inspiration for all artists, and especially painters.

1. *Avlaki.*
2. *The little port at Kamini.*
3. *Periptero.*

INSIDE the TOWN

*The Kountouriotis mansion,
which today operates as a museum.*

Next to the mansion of Pavlos Kountouriotis is the church of the Ypapanti (the All-Holy Virgin), which has a beautiful wood-carved iconostasis. From here, continuing in an eastwards direction among the pretty lanes, we will come to a small square. An old, but excellently-preserved, one-storey building behind the square catches our attention. This is the traditional pharmacy of **Rafalias** which, as a sign on one side says, was founded in 1890! It is a white building, with yellow door and window frames and plaster railings on the parapet of its roof, on top of which two flags fly, the Greek flag and the flag of the European Union. If it is impressive from the outside, then its inside is even more impressive. Nothing has changed inside since the 110 years that have passed since it was founded. The wooden shelves with the porcelain jars, the drawers with the white-enamel labels, on which the contents are written in black, Latin characters, even the pharmacist's little desk with the old 'accurate' scales set at the edge.

Miaoulis Street, the main road of Hydra, is only a short distance from this pharmacy, where it seems as though time has stopped since 1890. This is the road which leads into the town and terminates at **Kala Pigadia** (Good Wells), one of the oldest and prettiest neighbourhoods of Hydra. The name comes from two wells which are located there. Their parapets are whitened and are covered with a conical iron sheet that has been painted grey. Both are on a raised level, as the land rises here, which can be reached by climbing up six stone steps. These wells, which are over 200 years old, supply the residents of the old town with water.

The ascending road above Kala Pigadia leads up the hill of Kiafas, where Hydra's oldest quarter is built. The beautiful church of Ayios Konstantinos the Hydraiot stands tall almost at the top of the hill, at the point where the Saint was martyred. It celebrates its feast day on 14 November, when there is a festival. There is another church in **Kiafas** which is considered to be one of the oldest in the whole island. This is Ai-Yiannis, with its wonderful wall paintings.

After the tour of the port and the walk from Periptero to Kaminia, the visitor can now get to know the inside of the town. The best way to do this is to start at Lignos Street, which is on the right of the Monastiri, turning right a little further down to visit the historic house of **Lazaros Kountouriotis**. This is now an annex of the National Historical Museum in Athens. Lazaros Kountouriotis was an important historical figure during the Struggle of 1821. His house was built at the end of the 18th century and is a characteristic example of traditional Hydraiot architecture. In its halls today, one can see old island furniture next to console tables and buffets of the same period which the captains brought back with them from abroad, old English and Italian dinner sets, the personal items of Pavlos Kountouriotis, bronze kitchen equipment, baking trays, etc.

On the first floor of this mansion are exhibited, amongst other things, representative works of modern Greek art (18th-19th century) and the traditional costumes of the three main naval islands, Hydra, Spetses and Psara.

Monasteries of the Profitis Ilias and Ayia Evpraxia

The footpath which leads up to the monasteries of Profitis Ilias and Ayia Evpraxia starts at Kiafas. There is an asphalt-surfaced road for the monastery at Kala Pigadia, but this covers only a section of the route. The rest of it is made along a wide footpath, most of which passes through a thick pine forest. The mountain in front of the monasteries is bare, and the walker therefore has a chance to admire the wonderful view. Before him is the thick pine forest and down below is the port of Hydra. The white line of foam left behind by a speedboat can be seen floating on the blue sea, whilst the Peloponnesian coast opposite can be discerned. The pathway, which just before had quite a few bends as it clambered upwards, suddenly becomes a never-

1. The traditional pharmacy of Rafalias.
2. Kala Pigadia.
3. The town of Hydra.

ending stone stairway leading up in a straight path to the entrance of the Monastery of the Profitis Ilias. After a strenuous ascent, the grand entrance to the monastery, with the dome above the door and its gold wall painting, begins to stand out. I do not know why, but this last section of the road brings to mind a painting of a stairway shaped by the Houris of Paradise, a never-ending staircase which leads up into the sky where it becomes lost in its white light.

The visitors to the Monastery are most welcome, and are given a tour around it by one of the monks. The forecourt around the cathedral church and the monks' cells is huge. A cell in the north-west corner of the Monastery immediately grabs our attention. This is where Theodoros Kolokotronis, commander-in-chief of the Revolution of 1821, was gaoled for four months in that same year by his own fellow fighters. What injustice, what great destruction division can wreak! The monastery, built at a height of 500 metres, was founded in 1815.

Near the Monastery of Profitis Ilias is the Convent of Ayia Evpraxia, the female Saint of Good Acts. It was founded in 1821 and today has only one nun. Mountain climbers can ascend to the top of Mt Eros from the Monasteries. At 588 metres, this is the tallest mountain on Hydra and lies further to the south-west.

1. The monastery of Ayia Evpraxia.
2. The coastal settlement at Vlycho.

TOUR OF THE ISLAND

The tour of the island gives the visitor the opportunity to see not only the popular beaches, but also the other ones, those which are as equally delightful yet, because they are further from the port of Hydra, there might be only one swimmer in their waters.

This tour, which is made by the 'sea taxis,' as they are known, can commence in a westerly direction, where there is more of interest. The greatest disadvantage of these speedboats is their speed, which means that you do not really get a chance to properly enjoy the areas that you will pass. Another disadvantage is that they travel at a distance from the coasts that you wish to see. Both these disadvantages can be overcome by asking the driver to draw up close at any beach you wish to see and even to stop at some of these for a while. But, this must be agreed upon before you start.

The speedboat begins, then, from the port of Hydra, goes around the breakwater and proceeds towards Avlaki and pretty Kaminia, which we saw above. The new feature of this route will soon appear. It is **Vlychos**, a coastal settlement, built on the slope of a pretty mountain. A crowd of freshly-whitened little houses is located on a small, rocky hill, which protrudes into the sea, giving the landscape a special charm. Next to this small hill there is an organised beach with brown sand and deckchairs protected from the sun by large, straw umbrellas.

The next beach after Vlychos is **Palamidas**, with a large, old building to the left with a few boats, protected behind a dyke built next to the sea.

The little church of Ayios Kyprianos (St Cyprian) just beyond Palamida appears a brilliant white on a deserted beach with rocks and crystal-clear waters. After Ayios Kyprianos comes *Molos*, a large beach with a wonderful pine forest running along its whole length. Behind the pines is a steep cliff, and in front of the beach to the left is a walled estate with old, freshly-whitened one-storey houses and a few summer houses. From Molos, a road which cuts through the densest of the island's few pine forests, leads to *Episkopi*. There was a settlement in this area in prehistoric times, only a few of the remains of which survive. Today there are a few summer houses.

The speedboat continues the tour of the island, passing next alongside *Kaoumithi*, with the beautiful and verdant slopes which cut suddenly into the sea. Next, we come to the beach of Ayios Georgios at Bisti, near the bay of the same name. This beach has crystal-clear waters and is located in between two hills full of pine trees. The little church of *Ayios Georgios* dominates on the rocks to the left. There is a small forecourt in front of its entrance, which leads to a stone staircase with five or six steps. Practically all the surfaces are white: the church, the parapet in the forecourt, the dry

stone wall opposite. Only the door and window frames, the floor of the forecourt, and the tops of the steps are painted blue. From this little church one can better enjoy a view of this delightful bay. Some boats tied up on the rocks below add their own touch to the charm of the landscape.

After Bitsi and its bay, the direction of our route changes and we begin to travel in an easterly direction. *Ayios Nikolaos*, a pebbly beach, is relatively close by. There is a large gulf at its cove with rocks to the right and a forest further in. The crystal-clear waters and absolute calm invite us in for a swim. Without a doubt, one can swim at Ayios Nikolaos with the certainty that they will be the only one. The only other presence might be a fishing caique resting on the calm waters.

The same is true at the next beach, *Nisiza*, with the rocks to the right, the brown mountain and the vegetation further in. It is said that the port of the ancient settlement of Episkopi was here. Continuing our course, the landscape becomes more bare, when, suddenly, the Spilia tis Fokas - the cave of the seal - appears, followed by the pretty little church of Ayios Nikolaos Rigas, just before the cape of the

1

2

3

125

same name. Built on a rise above the brown rocks next to the sea, there are some small unapproachable bays full of rocks to the right and the left. After the pass from the cape of Rigas, the direction has now changed to a northerly one, soon reaching **Limnioniza**, the most interesting beach on this side of the island. The first sight of the rocks at the entrance and the large sandy beach with its crystal-clear waters is enough to take your breath away. The most beautiful thing, however, is the rocky islet in the centre, with its stunning colours and the sea all around it.

There are only a few people here, those who have come by caique or speedboat. There are also some, only a few of course, who have come here from Hydra town by foot, walking for two hours in order to enjoy this beautiful beach. Above Limnioniza, at a distance from it, is the Convent of Ayios Nikolaos.

In order to continue our little journey we must pass the cape of Zourva, the most easterly point of the island. The Monastery of Zourva soon appears, the most isolated of all on the island, at a distance of three and a half hours from Hydra town. Unless you come by boat, in which case you can moor beneath the Monastery and then walk for 45 minutes to reach it.

The tour of the island will end with a visit to **Mantraki**, also known as Mirmare, which is 20 minutes from the port of Hydra, or 5 minutes if you take one of the regular speedboat connections.

This was the military port of the Hydraiots during the years of the War of Independence. The bay which we find ourselves in is surrounded by bare and rocky mountains, with beautiful sands at its cove. The tourist complex of Mirmare is here. Thanks to its organised beach, it has much to offer visitors for an enjoyable swim and also the chance to indulge in some water sports. Next to the cafe and restaurant is the landing-stage for the boats which come and go from the port of Hydra.

The return journey to Hydra is short, just as the tour of the island with the speedboat was relatively short. Yet, within this brief time, the visitor has had a chance to see the beauties

hidden in the island's beaches. He or she will return from this experience full of satisfaction. A satisfaction which leads to one particular desire: to come again.

1. Mantraki.
2. The beach at Nisiza.
3. The beach at Limnioniza.

SPETSES

This island at the entrance of the Argosaronic has its own charms. There are no bare mountains, as in Hydra. Instead, Spetses has green hills which slope gently down towards the sea. The horizon is open, and the colours of the light shine unimpeded, filling the place with life.

The town of Spetses spreads out lazily along the length of the beach, only rising gradually in the centre, towards Kastelli, where the first inhabitants of the island chose to settle.

Below Kastelli is the famous port of Dapias, with the raised beach and the cannons which protected the island from attack by the Turks during the Revolution of 1821.

Behind Dapias are some of the town's finest mansions and below, just off the centre of a giant square to the right, proudly stands the bronze statue of the heroine Bouboulina, who gave her all to the Struggle of 1821. Bouboulina was the legendary female captain, who started off with her ships from the island to

The Island of Bouboulina

besiege Nafplion and Monemvasia. After this, charging along on a white horse, she was the first to enter Tripolitsa as it was being freed from the Turkish yoke.

To the south of Dapias is the pretty Palio Limani, the Old Port, with the old shipyards. Here some Spetsiots still continue the ancient craft of wood carving, and the Old Port adds its own touch to the town of Spetses. The town is, without a doubt, the main point of attraction for visitors. Yet, the town has one more great advantage: its wonderful beaches. The spacious Ayii Anargyri and the wonderful Ayia Paraskevi on the south coast, with Zogeria and Vrellos, where the sea takes on amazing colours, on the north coast. This combination, along with the excellent tourist facilities, have made Spetses so beloved, that the island is deluged with tourists in the summer.

Geography

Spetses lies to the right of the entrance of the Argosaronic Gulf, and only 1.5 nautical miles from the Peloponnesian coast. The island is oval-shaped, with a surface area of 22 square kilometres, and a population of almost 4000, most of which lives in the town of Spetses. The island is 52 nautical miles from the port of Piraeus, with which there are daily connections. To the south-east of Spetses, and very close by, is the luscious-green private island of Spetsopoula.

Morphology

The island is covered in dense pine forest, with relatively low hills, the tallest of which is Profitis Ilias (252 metres) in the centre of the island. The coastline is full of large and small bays, the principal ones being Ayia Marina in the east of the island where there is also a summer resort, Xylokeriza, the large bay of the Ayii Anargyri with the organised beach and summer houses, Ayia Paraskevi - these are all on the south and south-west coast - and Zogeria and Vrellos on the island's north coast.

CAPE VAIZA

VRELOS BEACH

CAPE ZOGERIA

ZOGERIA BAY

Agios Georgios

FRANGIAS

CAPE KAMARES

Vrelos

Analipsis

Zogeria

MT. BOURBOULO

BOURBOULO

CAPE FOIKES

MT. TOURLORAHI

22 +

KORMBI BAY

Agia Paraskevi

Agia Paraskevi

CAPE TSAKONAS

TOULOUMI

AGIA PARASKEVI BAY

CAPE TOULOUMI

Agii Anargiri

Agii Anargiri

AGII ANARGIRI BAY

CAPE KASIDOKAVOS

ELENIS BAY

CAPE ASTAKOKAVOS

CAPE HONDROKAVO

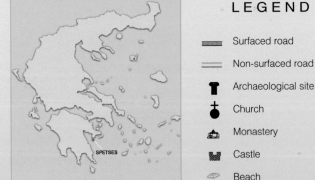

SPETSES

LEGEND

▬	Surfaced road
═	Non-surfaced road
♆	Archaeological site
☦	Church
⛪	Monastery
♜	Castle
⛱	Beach
⋀	Camp site

XO

X

SPETSES

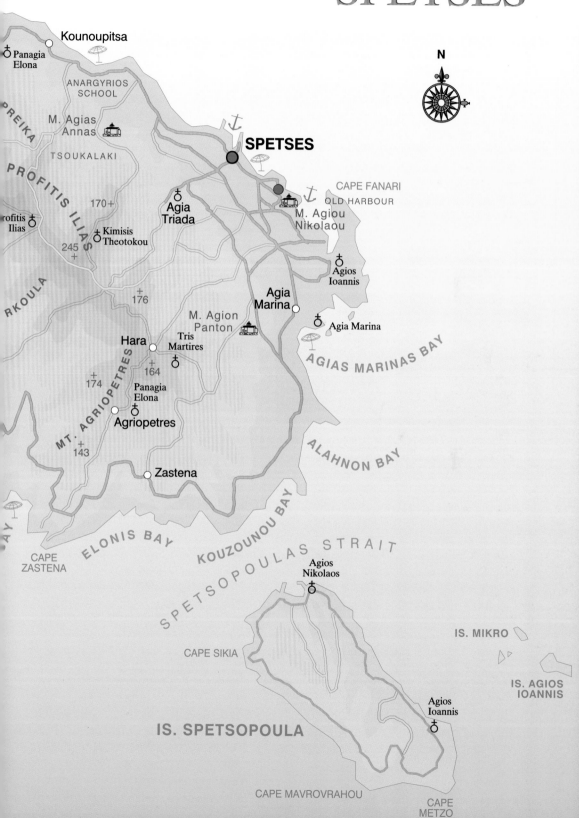

N

Panagia
Elona

Kounoupitsa

PREIKA

ANARGYRIOS
SCHOOL

M. Agias
Annas

TSOUKALAKI

PROFITIS ILIAS

170+

rofitis
Ilias

245
+

RKOULA

SPETSES

CAPE FANARI

Agia
Triada

Kimisis
Theotokou

176
+

M. Agiou
Nikolaou

OLD HARBOUR

Agios
Ioannis

M. Agion
Panton

Agia
Marina

Hara

Tris
Martires

164

Agia Marina

AGIAS MARINAS BAY

174
+

MT. AGRIOPETRES

Panagia
Elona

Agriopetres

143
+

ALAHNON BAY

Zastena

AY

ELONIS BAY

CAPE
ZASTENA

KOUZOUNOU BAY

SPETSOPOULAS STRAIT

Agios
Nikolaos

IS. MIKRO

CAPE SIKIA

IS. AGIOS
IOANNIS

IS. SPETSOPOULA

Agios
Ioannis

CAPE MAVROVRAHOU

CAPE
METZO

MYTHOLOGY & HISTORY

In ancient times the island was known as Pity-ousa, i.e. pine-tree island. The island was inhabited in the Early Bronze Age (3rd millennium BC), as we can see from the finds at Ayia Marina. Older finds have been located in the region of Zogeria, such as a stone tool from the Mesolithic period and Neolithic arrow heads, all of which are now in the collection of the Museum of Spetses. Even so, it appears that the sites at which these artefacts were found were not perma-nent settlements in these periods, and so these arte-facts were possibly left by visitors from the neigh-bouring Peloponnese.

There is very little evidence for the periods which followed. From this we can conclude that the island had few occupants and that it was dependent upon the neighbouring cities of the Peloponnese. On the other hand, there are finds that prove that the island was inhabited during the later Roman and Byzantine periods, just as it is also known that the Venetians took over the island in 1204, calling it the Isola di Spezzie, i.e. the aromatic island. It is possible that today's name of Spetses, or Spetsai, derives from this, but the most generally accepted opinion is that it comes from 'pitys,' i.e. pine.

The Turks conquered the Peloponnese in 1460. A few years later the first Arvanites, Orthodox Christians of Albanian descent, began to arrive on the island. They were refugees attempting to escape Turkish persecution. The Arvanites were soon followed by Greeks from the Argolid, Hermione, Kynouria and Laconia, who were fleeing for the same reason. They lived together peacefully. Their common goal was to survive in a place that was free, far from the dynasts. The greatest danger they now had to face was the pirates.

They gathered together, then, on a hill, at a point which could not be seen from the sea, and built Kastelli there, on the ruins of a much earlier settlement.

In the beginning they rose livestock. Soon, however, they realised that the sea could offer them much more. Indeed, this was something that their neighbours on Hydra had already understood. So, they turned to fishing, something for which they needed ships. And in this too they were lucky, as their island was rich in pine trees, providing them with the raw materials with which to build their fishing boats.

The beginning was made with small boats, and they later progressed to building much larger ones. By the middle of the 18th century, then, Spetses had the second-largest fleet in the whole of Greece, after Hydra. With this fleet the Spetsiots, along with the Hydraiots, were able to control commercial shipping not only in the Greek seas, but throughout the whole Mediterranean.

In 1768, war broke out between Russia and the Ottoman Empire. The Russians sent Orloff to the Peloponnese in an effort to inspire a Greek uprising against the Turks. The events which took place in Greece at that time are today known as the 'Orlofika,' having taken their name from this Russian noble. In 1770, the Spetsiots came out on the side of the Russians, but the revolt failed and the Turkish reprisals were harsh. Kastelli was set alight and its inhabitants killed or imprisoned.

In 1774, the war between Russia and the Turks ended with the defeat of the Turks and the signing of the Treaty of Kutchuk Kaynarca. The Spetsiots were amnestied, they returned to their island and began to extend their town from Kastelli towards the coast. The Turks were obliged to open the straits of the Bosphorus, thus enabling free passage to the Black Sea. The Spetsiot captains took advantage of this, and, with Russian favour, now sailed towards the Black Sea. They shipped mainly wheat, not only to the whole of the Mediterranean, but even to the

Baltic countries and America. The wealth began to flow through to the island, and was to increase even more later as a result of further developments.

The French Revolution broke out in 1769, and later the war between Britain and Napoleon. The British blocked the Mediterranean, but the only people who were brave enough to break through this blockade were the Hydraiots and the Spetsiots. Control of shipping was now in their hands.

We are now at the beginning of the 19th century, and the idea of a Greek revolution has become rooted deeply in the hearts of the Greeks. The territory had been prepared by the 'Filiki Etairia,' the Friendly Society, a secret revolutionary organisation whose members numbered leading Greek figures, including many Spetsiots. On 3 April 1821, then, Spetses became the first island of the Argosaronic to join the Revolution. Its fleet included fifty large ships and twenty-five smaller ones, all equipped with powerful cannons. Among these ships were those of the heroine Laskarina Bouboulina, her largest ship the 'Agamemnon,' in which she herself sailed, leading the Spetsiot fleet. The achievements of this fleet, which united with those of Hydra and Psara under the command of Andreas Miaoulis, were so great that it would require a whole book in which to detail them. Here we shall refer to only the most important.

There were two garrisons in the Peloponnese that were in Turkish hands. These were at Monemvasia and Nafplion. Bouboulina was charged with blocking these off with her fleet. The blockade lasted for many years, but it was decisive and it was only because of Bouboulina's efforts that the two fortresses finally fell to the Greeks. Bouboulina did not just stick to the war at sea. Along with her brave, young men, she participated in the siege of the main town in the Peloponnese at the time, Tripolitsa.

All this happened in 1821, the year in which the War of Independence broke out. And the achievements of the Spetsiot fleet in the following years were as equally great. In 1822, it chased the Turkish fleet all the way to Souda in Crete; in 1824 it

Exhibits in the Museum of Spetses.

rushed to help the people of Kasos, Psara and Samos; in 1825 came the victorious battle at Kafereus. Also impressive were the occasions when the Turkish fleet was fired upon by Spetsiot fireships, especially the naval engagement that took place on 8 September 1822, and which is celebrated annually on Spetses with a regatta.

The close of the War found the Spetsiots having used up all their wealth for the Revolution, and they were in very dire economic straits. The island kept up a little marine activity until the mid-19th century, when the final decline set in and the population of Spetses began to fall. A whole century needed to pass before the island could be brought back to life again with the development of tourism.

Typical lane in the town of Hydra.

YESTERDAY
& TODAY

People: *The Spetsiots and the Hydraiots have many things in common. This is, of course, not at all surprising, since their ancestors, the first people to settle on both islands, were Arvanites. The fact that Greeks also arrived a little after these first settlers does not really make much difference. The two people share the same fate. Both Arvanites and Greeks came from the Peloponnese to escape Turkish persecution. Their struggle from that point on was the same, to survive. We shall not distinguish between them. Both love freedom. They are rebellious, brave, adventurous, stubborn, honourable. They demonstrated all these characteristics during the Ottoman period, and even more during the years of the Struggle for Liberation. As soon as the mayhem of the war passed and Greece was free thanks to their heroic efforts, they could then show another side to their character: their gentle and peaceful side, their sweet and calm side. The women helped greatly during the difficult years. They stood by their men during the Struggle, yet in the home they remained ideal home-makers and true noble women.*

The Hydraiots have the same character more or less, yet both sets of islanders love the sea to such a great degree that it is difficult to say which of the two loves it more. This love of the sea is what first turned the Spetsiots to fishing, and later to shipping and trade. And it was this love that first made them wealthy and, along with the Hydraiots, masters of the Mediterranean, allowing them to play such a leading role in the liberation of Greece. The Spetsiots know this for themselves, and are proud of the fact. They may have given their all to the Struggle, to have sacrificed their whole wealth for it, and to have come out of this victorious battle wretched and poor, but they did not regret what they did, and would certainly do the same again. The visitor can sense this from the moment that he steps foot on the island.

He can sense this national exhaltation everywhere. From the monuments, the people, the smell of the air itself. All start and end from the sea, the struggles of the locals for their freedom, and for the sake of freedom. The Spetsiots may be more involved with tourism now, this is where most of their income comes from. But their old love for the sea has not disappeared. Their second source of income is shipping and fishing. Further down, the visitor will encounter the old keels and shipyards, there where in the 18th century the Spetsiots built their famous merchant vessels. Yet, he will be even more surprised when he sees that at four or five of these 'shipbuilders,' they are still building and repairing wooden ships.

Customs: *Just as the Spetsiots' love of the sea has not extinguished, neither has their dedication to their local customs. They might not have adhered to the traditions so much in recent years, but today there is a trend towards reviving these local customs. One of these is the **wedding**, which on Spetses, as in most parts of Greece, is an entire 'ritual' lasting for several days. It begins with the cleaning out of the house in which the couple is going to live, to which the bride's dowry is then brought. It is accompanied by musical*

instruments - violin and lute - which lead the procession. There follows the custom of the 'making of the bed,' when friends visit the couple and leave their gifts upon the bridal bed. As might be expected, the wedding day itself is of the greatest interest. The bride is dressed in her home in the company of her friends, who sing as they take care of her. At the same time, the groom is being prepared in his own home. There is a special feature to this custom, the so-called 'barber's toast.' The barber, who has really to put his skills to the test in order to prepare the groom as best he can, is offered plenty of sweets and a very rich tip. The ritual begins with the best man, who along with the 'violia' (the musical accompaniment of violin and lute), is the first to go and get the groom, along with the guests, in order to go to the house of the bride. A rug has been laid out at the front door of the house, and the groom must step on it to enter. At the entrance they are offered a spoon of 'pelte' (quince preserve). The groom takes the bride and, along with the local instruments which always lead the procession, they go to the church, singing a couplet known throughout almost the whole of Greece:

*"Today there is a wedding
in a beautiful orchard.
Today the mother
is to be separated from her daughter."*

After the wedding ceremony, almond sweets, soumada (an almond drink), and svingos (home-made sweet fritters) are offered. The formal wedding reception takes place in the evening, where the splendid special breads known as 'petes' are offered. 'Petes' are made with various aromatic spices (cinnamon, cloves, orange peel, bay leaves) and decorated with little flags and various goodies. After the drinking and eating comes the dancing and song, to the accompaniment of local instruments.

In the old days, in addition to the violin and the lute there was also the santouri, a kind of dulcimer. With their music, these instruments gave the cue for the singing and dancing. The folk songs on Spetses come from the Aegean islands and the Peloponnese next door. There are very few locally-produced folk songs. We quote here from one of these pieces, which talks of a local spot on Spetses:

*"At Bouboulos' wickers,
I kissed you, but do not tell."*

As for the dances, there are the island ballos (danced by couples) and the syrtos (a group dance), as well as the Peloponnesian Kalamatianos (a circle dance), which features over almost all of Greece, and many others.

One can enjoy Spetsiot music and dance at the island's festivals. These had begun to die out, but today there is a movement for their revival. The main ones are: the festival of Ai-Yiorgis at Zogeria on 23 April, Zoodochos Pigi (after Easter) at the churches of Elonas, on 1 July at the Ayii Anargyri, the last Sunday of the Easter Carnival at Roloi Square, and on Clean Monday at Sourbouti and Kastelli. The anniversary of the naval battle of Spetses is celebrated on 8 September at the church of Panayia tin Armata (Virgin Mary of the Fleet) with events lasting for several days, ending with a live reconstruction of the firing of the Turkish fleet and a fireworks display.

One might expect at these festivals to see the traditional Spetsiot costume being worn, but this only appears at the odd cultural event. And this is a pity, because the beauty of this dress competes only with

that of Salamis, which is famed for its luxury and elegance.

Architecture: We have already touched upon the architecture of the island in our discussion of the mansions of Bouboulina and Sotiris Anargyros in the town of Spetses. The former represents the old mansion style, with its simple design, external staircase of stone, the courtyard with the tall walls and also the interior with its wooden decor and rich furnishings. The latter mansion represents the newer buildings of the neo-classical style.

Arts and letters: As for the arts and letters, we can start by mentioning the old historians Anargyros Hadjianargyrou and Anastasios K. Orlandos, the professor and member of the Athens Academy Georgios Sotiriou, the first great Greek female painter Eleni Altamourou-Boukouri, her son Yiannis Altamouras, also a painter, the poets Georgios Stratigis, Yiannis Pergialitis, Maria Botsi, Giorgos Logothetis and Kostas Kokrovic. We will end by mentioning the contemporary painters Byron Kesses, Voula Mathew-Kourouzi, Petros Argyris, the folk painter Nikos Mantas and the poet Captain Lefteris Marmatsouris.

Local cuisine: It would be a serious omission not to say a couple of words about the local cuisine. Most people believe that the island's only dish is fish 'a la Spetstiota.' The locals, however, tend to disagree and would suggest that the visitor tries some meat with quince, beef with chunky macaroni and Tsakonian (from Tsakonia in the Peloponnese opposite) myzithra cheese, and 'propyra' (first fire), a bread made of wheat which is similar to the traditional 'lagana' Easter bread, yet to which salt and pepper have been added.

THE TOWN OF SPETSES

The town of Spetses is wonderfully charming. Its old three-storey houses with their simple design next to the sea are evocative of the nobility of Hydra. Only here, there are no naked and precipitous mountains all around to the give the town a grandiose air. The hills here are low and covered in vegetation, creating a calm and idyllic picture.

*Spetses welcomes its visitors at the historic **port of Dapias**. With its linear, raised pier, from the platform of which eight cannons lined in a row jut out. These are the same cannons that protected the town from the Turks during the Revolution of 1821. This picture intimates that here, just like in Hydra, the memories of that period still remain fresh. Even if over 180 years have passed since then.*

The boats moor a little past the entrance to the port, on the left. In front of the dock is a large, old building which is the home of the Port Authority. The 'sea taxis' are moored a little further up. This is what the speedboats which await their customers in order to transport them to the island's beautiful coasts and to those of the Peloponnese opposite are called. And, just as in Hydra, the little flag of the Revolution is a prerequisite on the sea taxis, placed alongside the Greek flag. These taxis, along with the horse-drawn carriages, are the only means of transport on the island, since cars are banned. From the piazza with the taxis onwards the road climbs up, soon reaching the raised section that we mentioned earlier. This is where most of the town's cafes are, jammed in together, with their little tables on the pebbly road in front of the sea. A road that, for all its length and breadth, is laid with white and dark green pebbles which form different patterns. This kind of decoration, which requires much time and effort, is a centuries' old tradition on Spetses. We shall also see this pebbled flooring in the squares, courtyards and the pathways of the gardens of the mansions. This road, which continues left and right from the port, is the town's main road. Full of shops, restaurants, pizza parlours and bars, it hustles and bustles, especially during the summer months.

Behind Dapias is Bouboulina Square, with its

pebbled floor and the bust of Bouboulina, the island's heroine, in the centre. In the front of the square the **mansion of Sotiris Anargyros**, a leading entrepreneur in both Europe and America, stands proud. Anargyros amassed a great fortune and then returned to his homeland of Spetses, where he built many important buildings and became the island's great patron. His mansion, a wonderful example of the neo-classical order, is a two-storey building with large verandas all around. The veranda on the upper floor was supported by columns which created a peristyle. A pebbled pathway with beautiful patterns and lined with palm trees leads, through the garden, to the entrance to the mansion.

1. The mansion of Sotiris Anargyros.
2, 3, 4, 5. External view of the Museum of Spetses and views of the exhibition area.

Mansion houses today functioning as Museums

The splendid **mansion** that belonged to **Laskarina Bouboulina** stands to the right of Sotiris Anargyros' mansion. The heroine of Spetses played an important role in the Struggle of 1821. Not just because she dedicated her entire wealth to building and arming war ships, but because she led the fleet herself, taking part in many battles. Among these were the sieges with her fleet of Nafplion and Monemvasia, which were occupied by the Turks, and the liberation of Tripolitsa. The Greek chieftains and her fellow fighters gave her the titles of Capetanissa (Lady Captain) and Great Lady. After her death, Russia, under whose flag her merchant fleet sailed before the Revolution, bestowed upon her the honorary title of Admiral. Bouboulina, then, is the only women in the world to have received this title.

In contrast to the mansion of Sotiris Anargyros, the mansion of Bouboulina is simple and in total harmony with the other old mansions, yet without lacking in grandeur. Today it operates as a museum, complete with a guided tour which is

1

2 given in English and Greek. The visitor will have the chance to see, amongst other things, the large wooden sitting room with its carved, wooden Florentine ceiling and the Florentine furniture, as well as the huge safe of the ship 'Agamemnon,' the flagship of its fleet, and the dining room with a beautiful icon of St Nicholas dating from 1811. Also on exhibition are Bouboulina's gun, with its carved handle, and her silk kerchief, embroidered with gold and silver.

3   Near the mansion of Bouboulina is another old mansion house, which once belonged to Hadjiyiannis Mexis, one of the island's leading notables during the great Struggle of 1821. This mansion was built between 1795 and 1798 with wings on both sides, and has a ground floor plus two further floors. Arched stoas in the building's facade lighten somewhat its heavy structure. Mexis' own private rooms were on the ground floor, whilst the women's and guests' rooms were on the first floor, and the 'great ontas' - room in Turkish - which was used as a function room by the family during the years of

4 the Revolution was on the second floor.
    The Museum is today housed on the first floor, which has eight rooms. The first contains exhibits relating to the island's nautical tradition, including the wooden figure-heads from ships. The second room houses archaeological finds. Of especial interest are the so-called 'gravy trays,' spouted bottles from the proto-Helladic settlement at Ayia Marina. The third room is host to a collection of Byzantine and post-Byzantine icons. Two old maps are on display in the fourth room. The first is a map of Spetses

5 that was published in 1896 and the other is a large map of Greece dating from 1884. The fifth room houses a collection of Eastern and European ceramics which had been brought to the island by Spetsiot sailors. Traditional costumes are on display in the sixth room. Amongst them stands out the bridal gown of the noble woman Anesto Lembesi.
    Finally, the seventh room houses the actual flag of the Revolution of 1821, sailors' weapons, portraits and the bones of Laskarina Bouboulina.

The Monastery of Ayios Nikolaos.

The Palio Limani (Baltitza).

From Dapia to the Old Port (Baltiza)

From Dapias, the central road continues in a south-east direction, parallel with the coast. It soon arrives at a sandy beach, a little before the church of Ayios Mamas. This is the nearest beach where you can swim, and it attracts many people in the summer. This is also the bus stop from which the buses which run the few connections for the island's distant beaches leave.

A little beyond Ayios Mamas, higher up than the sea, is the elegant building of the Capodistrian Cultural Centre of Spetses, which was recently repaired and renovated. It is painted white, with grey doors and grey steps. There is plaster decoration and the roof contains two pediments, on both the front and back, giving it the air of an ancient temple. The splendid **Monastery of Ayios Nikolaos** is about 300 metres from the Cultural Centre, with its tall belfry and giant pebbled forecourt. Its cathedral church, today the Metropolitan church of Spetses, was built in 1805. It is a cruciform-style church with a dome, and next to it is a smaller church dedicated to three Spetsiot martyrs. The Monastery, freshly painted and

well-cared for, looks over the sea from high up.

The coastal road that goes to the **Old Port** (Baltiza) passes beneath Ayios Nikolaos. Here, in the small bay formed beneath the monastery and the tall mansions, there is a pretty beach with blue-green waters. It is small, with fine pebbles and sand, and a few rocks at the edges. Here, swimmers can enjoy not just the waters but also the wonderful landscape.

The road continues around Ayios Nikolaos at this point and, having made a turn of 180 degrees, comes to the entrance of the Old Port. At the same moment, a new world, strange and idyllic, makes its appearance. Long and narrow, the bay of the Old Port seems to be endless. Countless colourful boats are anchored around it, from small boats to caiques and yachts.

There are houses all around, large and small, with old mansions scattered in between them. A pier standing at the start of the bay juts out a little into the sea. This pier was built for two reasons: in order to protect the port from the waves, but

The shipyards at the Palio Limani.

mainly so that large vessels could be moored to it. It is located opposite the lighthouse, which stands at the opposite side of the port. The dry land in the centre of the port slopes upwards a little. The houses at this point are built on both sides of the port, leaving a space for a small copse next to the beach, where the war memorial has been erected.

As the road continues towards the mouth of the port, the picture become even more enchanting. Tavernas and ouzo bars offering fresh fish and other goodies are now added to the scene. The horse-drawn carriages come and go, transporting visitors to the tavernas or the sights of the port. This is where most of the mansions are situated, built by local or even Italian craftsmen. Among them stand out those of Botasis, Goumas and Vamvas. From here, a road to the right leads to the church of the Analapsi (Ascension of Christ) and the district of the same name. The coastal road, which has now reached the cove of the bay, gradually begins to turn towards the opposite direction, to the side of the Faros, as the lighthouse is called.

The first shipyards, where they repair the wooden ships, now make their appearance. In one of these,

a large boat has been pulled out onto the sands. Its hull rests upon the wooden keels and it is held upright by wooden posts placed into the ground at its sides. There is a hole in the side which needs to be sealed, the masts have to be positioned, and the boat needs painting. This red does not seem to be its final colour. Further down from the shipyards are the old naval dockyards, where the Spetsiots built their merchant fleet in which they sailed throughout the whole Mediterranean.

The technique of ship building is ancient. Its roots lie not just in the days when the ancient Greeks built their famous triremes, but reach as far back as the Bronze Age. There are four or five small dockyards in the Old Port today, which continue the centuries' old tradition. On a large part of the eastern side of the port, then, one can see some wooden ships, the great majority of which are old, pulled up onto the dry land to await their turn for repair or maintenance.
It is doubtful whether you will be to see such a sight, with so many such ships, anywhere else in Greece.

The road now passes the naval dockyards and

enters a small pine forest. A little church painted yellow with a courtyard all around it somewhere to the right, grabs our attention. This is the **Panayia i Armata**, the Virgin Mary of the Fleet, built as a reminder of the Greek fleet's victorious battle against the Turkish fleet in the straits between Spetses and the Argolid on 8 September 1822. It is also a reminder of how the Panayia also saved the Spetsiots on that day. The danger arose when the Turkish fleet suddenly turned towards Spetses with the aim of landing there. There were only a few people on the island able to defend it, and their chances of withstanding the threat nil. It was then, as most Spetsiots believe, that the Panayia helped them to think of a truly clever solution. They placed a large number red fesia (caps) on top of some bushes in the area of the lighthouse. The Turks were deceived and believed that there was a large army on the island ready to defend it, so they did not attempt to land. This victory was also a redemption, and the Spetsiots celebrate its anniversary on 8 September each year - also the birthday of the Panayia - with much fanfare. There is a re-enactment of the naval battle in the evening, when a reconstruction of the Turkish flag ship is fired. The celebration ends with fireworks, which fill the sky.

The firing of the Turkish command ship during this historic naval battle was the decisive factor in the Greek victory. The brave fighter who managed to approach the Turkish ship and to set fire to it was the Spetsiot Kosmas Barbatsis. His compatriots honour him as well, and have set up his bronze statue on the cannon station at Faros.

The lighthouse stands tall at the edge of the cape, in front of the entrance to the Old Port. The whole of this area has taken its name from the lighthouse, and is known as Faros, i.e. lighthouse in Greek. Next to the lighthouse are the installations of the military navy, and below this is the famous Peripatos (walk) along the cannon station. This is what they have called a park in front of the beach, about ten metres above the sea. The Peripatos is long and there are openings every four metres along its platform. These openings contain cannons, the same ones that protected the port during the Struggle of 1821. Behind the cannons, on top of a pile of stones, is the statue of Barbatsis. He holds a short staff in one hand and a torch in the other - the torch with which he set fire to the enemy's command ship. On the rise above the statue there stands a tall flagpole in between two cannons, with two flags at its

peak: the Greek and once again, the Spetsiot flag of the Revolution, with the words "Freedom or Death." Both flags flutter in the light breeze, as though they wanted to tell us that the past is not so distant from the present. That the memories of what happened on this island, and in particular in the straits between Spetses and the Peloponnese, are still fresh for the Spetsiots.

A strange composition in metal on the sea below, representing a gorgon, catches our attention. It was made by the same artist who created the statue of Bouboulina.

The walk in the park with the cannon station is very pleasant. One can sit for hours and enjoy the view of the Old Port, as seen from behind the cannons. If it is late in the afternoon, then one can remain here, in the little copse, until sunset. The sun will set behind the monastery of Ayios Nikolaos, adding a golden colour to the sea. And a glimpse of the gorgon can be caught, down on the beach, to the right.

1. The church of the Panayia Armata.
2. The statue of the gorgon.
3. The statue of Kosmas Barbatsis at the canon station.
4. The Greek flag and the flag of the revolution in between two canons at Faros.

Kastelli - Panayia Daskalaki
Profitis Ilias

Behind Dapias, at a distance of 500 metres from the sea, is **Kastelli**, the oldest neighbourhood in the town. It is built high up, on the site of a natural fortress, with a wonderful view over the town of Spetses and the surrounding region. It is situated in between two streams, which protect it at the sides: the stream of Ayios Georgios to the left and that of Kounoupitsa to the right.

It appears that the first inhabitants of the area chose this site on which to settle. The research which has been done shows that the first settlement dates to the classical period. Later, it was used as a refuge for people from Methana who had abandoned their houses after the eruption of the Methana volcano in 273 BC. From that point on we have no other extant reference to the settlement, until the arrival of the Arvanites, Christian Orthodox of Albanian descent, in the middle of the 16th century. They came from the Peloponnesian coasts opposite, persecuted by the

Turks, and many of them established a medieval settlement at Kastelli, on the site of the earlier settlement. By the beginning of the 17th century, then, Kastelli had evolved into a fully-developed settlement, with a fortification wall which it is said had seven gates. This settlement was the original core of the town which later expanded towards the sea.

All this took place during the Turkish occupation of Greece. During the war between Russia and Turkey from 1768 to 1774, the Spetsiots took part on the side of the Russians and rose up against the Turks. As a punishment, the Turks raided Spetses in 1770 and set fire to Kastelli, killing or imprisoning its inhabitants. The destruction of Kastelli by the Turks completed the deterioration already caused by the passage of time. Today, only three of the churches survive in the old city, whilst the houses all around are new.

The first church which the visitor shall encounter whilst walking up the narrow neighbourhood lanes is that of the **Ayia Triada** (Holy Trinity, late 18th

century), a three-aisled basilica with a dome and a wide belfry. Next comes the church of the Taxiarches (Archangels, early 19th century), a cruciform-style church with a dome and wall paintings. Both these churches are built in a simple style with thick walls. The third church is that of the **Koimisi tis Theotokou** (Dormition of the Virgin), a beautiful post-Byzantine cruciform-style church, with a dome and old wall paintings. This church is the oldest of the three, dating to the 17th century, and was the Metropolitan church of Spetses during the Revolution. The local chieftains swore their allegiance to the uprising in this church in 1822. Tradition mentions a miracle of the Panayia, the appearance of a giant spring with water, which saved the church from the fire that the Turks had set to it.

One can ascend directly to the wooded peaks of the island from Kastelli, although this is a little difficult as there is no specific footpath. The best solution is to follow the dirt road located close to the left, which eventually leads to the island's crest. This road, which is not really suitable for walking along, leads to the kiosk known as the 'hunters' meeting point.' A little further down is the **Panayia tou Daskalaki**, a little church built among the pine trees on the plateau formed at the peak of the mountain. The view from here over Kastelli, the rest of the island and the coasts of the Peloponnese opposite, is breathtaking. A little to the left is the peak of the Profitis Ilias, the island's highest. From the Profitis Ilias another dirt road leads down to the beach of Vrellos, which we shall mention again further down in the section on the tour of the island.

The neighbourhood of Kastelli.

1. The statue of Bouboulina.
2. The Poseidonio hotel.
3. The beach at Kounoupitsa.

From Dapia to Kounoupitsa

Beneath the cannon station of Dapia, to the right as we enter the port, there is a great square in front of the sea. In the south-west corner of the square stands the luxury Poseidonio hotel, an architectural master-piece of the early 20th century. With its large doors and windows, heavy iron railings around the balcony and columns at the entrance, it is one of the sights of Spetses most worth seeing. This hotel has hosted many important figures of the 20th century.

In the centre of the great square, which can be considered as the pier of the hotel, is the bronze stat-ue of Bouboulina, the heroine of the island and idol of all the Spetsiots. She has one hand reaching for the handle of her gun, which is bound around her waist, and the other raised to her forehead a little above the eyes, as though trying to spy some enemy ship sail-ing in the distance.

The walk along the beach of Kounoupitsa after the Poseidonio hotel is most enjoyable. Most of the houses were built after the Struggle of 1821, and the town of Spetses has expanded at a fast pace along the length of the beach. The greatest growth has been noted after the middle of the 20th century, with many luxury hotels, shops, tavernas and bars being built, making Kounoupitsa an attractive destination for tourists. Thankfully, in spite of the economic flurry, some old mansions have been preserved in among the new houses. These include Bouboulina's summer house, the mansion of Boukouras, the Town Hall - the white building with the roofed, domed entrance and the pink oleander, which was initially also a residential mansion. The old, abandoned Daskalakis textile factory is interesting, a rare example of industrial architecture.

After Kounoupitsa comes the village of Sourbouti, although the border between the two is not especially clear. Sourbouti can also be considered as the edge of Spetses town, and here the buildings begin to peter out. And yet, this last part of the town has many interesting features. The fine complex of the Anargyrios and Korgialenios School is to be found here, another creation of Sotiris Anargyrou, which operated for almost 50 years from 1927. This school, something akin to today's colleges, was considered one of the best in Europe and for this reason counted many non-Greeks among its pupils. In front of the school is the pretty copse which separates it from yet another of the beautiful organised beaches. It is located at a spot where the sand is drawn out, forming a tongue within the sea.

There are other beaches at which you can take a swim along this walk from Dapias to Kounoupitsa. There is one in front of the first houses of Kounoupitsa, and another between Kounoupitsa and Sourbouti. But, the beach in front of the school is the best, and in terms of the natural surroundings as well, as it is far from the noisy town. From here, Dapias and Faros can only just be seen, like distance capes within the turquoise sea.

1. The beach of Ayia Marina. 2. The beach in front of the Anargyrios and Korgialenios School. 3. Xylokeriza. 4. The beach of Ayia Paraskevi.

TOUR OF THE ISLAND

Spetses is smaller than Hydra, with a shorter coastline, without this meaning that the coasts of Spetses lack any of the beauty of those of Hydra. On the contrary, these coasts hide the most idyllic beaches of the Argosaronic.

As on Hydra, the tour of the island is done by 'sea taxi' after an agreement with the owner of the boat. To stop off at one or more of the beaches might be expensive, what is important for the visitor though is not just to glance at these wonderful beaches, but to stay for a while, even for a little, and to properly enjoy them this way. To swim in their crystal-clear seas and to enjoy the sun whilst lying on the pebbles or warm sand. There is also another way in which to do this: to take the coach for, e.g., the beach of Ayii Anargyri at 11:00 or 12:30 in the morning and to return at 15:30 or 17:00 in the afternoon.

Our subject here, however, is the tour of the island, which will start from the port of Dapias in the direction of Faro. The visitor will have the opportunity at the beginning of this trip to see again some of the things he or she has already encountered. The old mansions in a row in front of the sea, the monastery of Ayios Nikolaos, the entrance to the Old Port. At Faros, the boat reaches very close to the lighthouse, turning at the cape. Just beyond this turn a little blue church set upon the rocks, in front of the sea, catches our attention. This is Ayios Demitrios. The journey now makes its way along the island's eastern beaches. A little after Ayios Demitrios, the boat approaches **Ayia Marina,** *an organised beach with pebbles and sand. The slopes of the mountain behind the sands are covered in pine and cypress trees. There are several villas built in among them, and at the peak of the hill stands the resplendent Convent of the Ayii Pantes (All Saints), with a few nuns in residence. A pre-Helladic settlement over 3000 years-old has been discovered at Ayia Marina, the finds from which are now in the Museum of Spetses (see the Town of Spetses).*

The journey continues initially towards the south and then towards the west. The luscious-green private island of Spetsopoula which belongs to the

family of a shipowner who has been a great benefactor to Spetses, can now be seen close by to the left. The next organised beach is that of **Xylokeriza.** *The thick pine forest that surrounded this little beach was burnt down a few years ago, and this has substantially reduced its charm. Today, only the beach's white sands and turquoise waters remain.*

Having covered almost half the tour of the island, the boat now turns towards the south-west, heading for the largest and most frequented beach on the island. This is the **Ayii Anargyri,** *its beautiful sands spread out to form a large and open petal. There are thick pine trees all around it, among which many villas have been built. Ayii Anargyri is an organised beach with many water sports facilities. At a short distance to the west of the beach is the cave of Mekiris, which acted as a refuge for the Spetsiots during the years of the Struggle against the Turks. The cave is located among some rocks before the sea, yet its entrance cannot be seen from the approaching craft.*

On the next bay after the Ayii Anargyri is **Ayia Paraskevi,** *the most delightful beach of Spetses. The bay at this point is very small and tighter than the previous one. The pine trees seem taller, more bushy at this bay, and there is not a villa in sight. The only building here is the brilliant-white church of*

The Ayii Anargyri.

Ayia Paraskevi on the south edge of the sands. Fortunately or unfortunately - this depends on your own personal preference - this beach is organised too. There are a few umbrellas and deck chairs, although fewer than those at Ayii Anargyri, and there is also a canteen.

Our circumnavigation of the island continues. The boat proceeds as far as the cape which makes up the most westerly point of the island. Here, it changes direction and turns slowly towards the east. Another beach will soon make its appearance within this closed bay. This is **Zogeria**, with the brown sand and the thick pine trees all around. This is also an organised beach, with a restaurant hidden inside the forest. At the start of the beach there is a small set of stairs where passengers embark and disembark and where small boats are also tied. Here, one can observe something which is quite common at the pier of the Old Port. One of the island's many old cannons is set up upright with the mouth buried deep in the earth. It is secured so well that it is used as a post to which the boats are tied. The cannon at the landing-place of Zogeria has been painted white, in contrast with those at the Old Port, which are completely black. Traces of a pre-Helladic settlement such as that at Ayia Marina have been found at the cape, which is located at the end of the bay.

Everything at Zogeria is very clean - the small landing-place, the sand, the restaurant - and the sea waters are crystal clear.

After Zogeria, the last beach that we will approach is the magical beach of **Vrellos**. The colours of the sea here are perhaps more beautiful than at any other of the island's beaches.

The slope of the land makes the lively pine trees literally hang over the narrow pebbly strip. A large flock of seagulls has found the opportunity, then, to rest for a while before continuing on its endless flight. Theirs is a persistent and endless quest for food, irrespective of whether this is to be found over a calm or a stormy sea.

We have already begun our return to the starting point. A few scattered villages start to appear on the right of the boat, far from the town of Spetses. Now, the parts that the traveller has already encountered during his or her tour overland: the beautiful beach in front of the Anargyirios and Korgialenios School full of swimmers, Kounoupitsa, the old mansions, the Poseidonio hotel, and, finally, the port of Dapias with the cannon station.

Our tour of the island by boat finishes here, and along with it our tour of Spetses, the luscious-green island with the glorious history.

1. The beach at Zogeria.
2. The beach of Vrellos.

USEFUL INFORMATION

How to Get There

For Aegina, Angistri, Poros, Hydra and Spetses take the boat or ferry from Piraeus (information: Piraeus Port Authority tel. 010 4593123). For a quicker journey, you can take the speedboat, again from Piraeus (from Akti Miaoulis or Zea). Information: Minoan Flying Dolphins, tel. 010 4199200. In addition to its main port, Aegina also has two other ports, Souvala and Ayia Marina, to which you can go directly from Piraeus by boat or speedboat, whilst you can also go to Angistri from Aegina. There are daily connections for all these journeys, with more daily connections in the summer and less in the winter.

You can even go by car to Poros, taking the National Highway for Corinth, and then the road for the Isthmos, Epidaurus and Galata. There are regular ferry boat connections to Poros from Galata.

You can also take your car to Spetses by following the same route, but after Nea Epidaurus, you must follow the new road for Koliaki, Kranidi and Kosta, which lies opposite Spetses. You must leave your car at Spetses because private vehicles are banned on the island, just as they are on Hydra too.

For Salamis (Paloukia, Selinia, Kamatero) you will take one of the many regular boat connections from Piraeus in the summer. You can also go by ferry boat, and there are many connections throughout the year from Perama (west of Piraeus) to Paloukia on Salamis.

Where to Stay

There are many hotels and rented rooms on all the islands of the Argosaronic, in both the main towns and the villages (Salamis has the fewest).

Local Public Transport

There are local buses on all the islands of the Argosaronic except Hydra. The two largest islands, Salamis and Aegina, have the most frequent connections.

USEFUL TELEPHONE NUMBERS

Salamis 010
Hospital 4677162
Health Centre 4651888
Police 4651100
Port Authority 4677277
Moulki 010
Municipal
district 4662243
Selenia 010
Municipal
district 4671510
Ambelakia 010
Taxis 4672292

Aegina 02970
Health Centre 22222
Police 23333
Tourist Police 27777
Port Authority 22328
Municipality 22220
Taxis 22635
Ayia Marina .... • .02970
Rural Doctor's Surgery 32175
Port Authority 32358
Perdika 02970
Municipal
district 61073

Angistri 02970
Rural Doctor's Surgery 91251
Police 91201
Community Offices ...91260
Poros 02980
Rural Doctor's Surgery 22600
Police 22256
Tourist Police 22462
Port Authority 22274
Municipality 22250
Taxis 23003
Hydra 02980

Hospital 53150
Rural Doctor's Surgery 52420
Police 52205
Tourist Police 52205
Port Authority 52279
Municipality 52210
Spetses 02980
Rural Doctor's Surgery 72472
Police 73100
Tourist Police 73744
Port Authority 72245
Municipality 72225
Μόνιππα 73171

HOTELS

AEGINA (02970)
AEGINITIKO ARCHONTIKO(A) ...24968
DANAI ....(B) 22424
MIRANDA ....(B) 22266
MICHAIL MARA ....(B) 26421
NAUSICA ....(B) 22333
AEGINA ....(C) 22472
ARETI ....(C) 23593
AVRA ....(C) 22303
KLONOS ....(C) 25874
NERINA ....(C) 23038
PAVLOU ....(C) 22795
ATHENA PAVLOU .....(D) 23011
ARTEMIS ....(D) 25195
MARMARINOS ....(D) 23510
PEPPAS ....(D) 23793
ULRIKA ....(E) 25600
TOYAH ....(E) 24242
CHRISTINA ....(E) 25600
Ayia Marina
APOLLO ....(B) 32271
ARGO ....(B) 32266
KATERINA ....(B) 32205
AIGLI ....(C) 32221
AKTI ....(C) 32249
AMOUDIA ....(C) 32213
APHAIA ....(C) 32227
GALANI ....(C) 32203
ERATO ....(C) 32592
HERMES 32411
ISIDORAS ....(C) 32414
CAROUSEL ....(C) 32496
KARAS ....(C) 32464
CARYATIDS ....(C) 32331
CLEOPATRA ....(C) 32038
KYRIAKIDES ....(C) 32588
LIBERTY ....(C) 32353
LIBERTY II ....(C) 32645
MAGDA ....(C) 32325
BLUE SUNDRIVE .....(C) 32646
BLUE HORIZON .....(C) 32303
NEKTARIOS ....(C) 32438
OASIS ....(C) 32312
OLYMPIAKI AGONES ...(C) 32110
PANORAMA ....(C) 32202
PANTELAROS ....(C) 32431
PICCADILY ....(C) 32646
POSEIDON ....(C) 32392
SANDY BEACH ....(C) 32149
TA TRIA ADELFIA (THREE BROTHERS)
.........(C) 32229

VILLA MARIOLIS ....(D) 32495
CAVOS ....(D) 32338
ALEXANDROS ....(E) 32365
ANTHI ....(E) 32565
ANGELA ....(E) 32556
DELPHINI ....(E) 32451
BAKOMITROA ....(E) 32442
MYRMIDON ....(E) 32558
RAUMA ....(E) 32168
Vaia
XENI ....(C) 71150
VAGIA ....(E) 71179
Perdikas
ILIOPERATO ....(C) 61455
SISSY (MARATHON) .....(D) 26222
MOODY BAY (Profitis Ilias) (B) ..61166
Souvala
EFI ....(C) 52214
SARONIKOS ....(D) 52224

ANGISTRI (02970)
Megalochori
MYLOS ....(D) 91241
AKTI ....(E) 91232
NONDAS ....(E) 91209
FLOISVOS ....(E) 91264
Skala
ANDREAS ....(D) 91346
GALINI ....(D) 91530
MANARAS ....(D) 91312
SARONIS ....(D) 91394
ANGISTRI ....(E) 91288
AKTAION ....(E) 91222
ALEXANDRA ....(E) 91251
ANAGENESIS ....(E) 91332
ANASTASIOU ....(E) 91317
ARTEMIS ....(E) 91309
YIANNA ....(E) 91228
MARY ....(E) 91421
PAGONA ....(E) 91122
POULAKIS ....(E) 91353

POROS (02980)
Dionysos ....(B) 23511
Latsi ....(B) 22392
Saron ....(B) 22279
Aktaion ....(C) 22281
Epta Adelfia (Seven Brothers) ......(C)
23412
Theano ....(C) 22567
Manesis ....(C) 22273

Dimitra ....(E) 22697
Pavlou (Neorio) ....(B) 22750
Poros (Neorio) ....(B) 22216
Anchor (Neorio) ....(C) 22368
Nea Aigli (Askeli) ....(B) 22372
Chrysi Avgi (Askeli) ....(C) 22277
Siren (Monastiri) ....(B) 22741

HYDRA (02980)
MIRANDA ....(A) 52230
BRATASERA ....(A) 53971
ORLOFF ....(A) 52564
ARES ....(B) 52564
GRECO ....(B) 53200
MISTRAL ....(B) 50509
SINTRA ....(B) 53401
HYDROUSSA ....(B) 52217
ANGELIKA ....(C) 53202
AMARYLLIS ....(C) 52249
DELPHINI ....(C) 52082
HIPPOKAMPOS ....(C) 53453
LITO ....(C) 53385
NEFELI ....(C) 53297
HYDRA ....(C) 52102
ARGO ....(D) 52452
DINA ....(D) 52248
SOFIA ....(D) 52213
Mantraki
MIRAMARE ....(B) 52300

SPETSES (02980)
Lefka Palace ....(A) 72311
Poseidonion ....(A) 72308
Spetses ....(A) 72602
Villa Christina ....(B) 72218
Roumanis ....(B) 72244
Armata ....(C) 72683
Villa Anesis ....(C) 73395
Villa Martha ....(C) 72147
Ilios ....(C) 72488
Star ....(C) 72214
Faros ....(C) 72613
Kamelia ....(D) 72415
Stelios ....(D) 73280
Alexandri ....(E) 73073
Anna-Maria ....(E) 73035
Margarita ....(E) 72027
Klimis ....(D) 73777
Argo ....(E) 73225
Ayii Anargyri
AKROYIALI ....B 73695

INDEX

BIBLIOGRAPHY

VASILIADIS, DEMETRIOS «Η λαϊκή αρχιτεκτονική της Αίγινας» ATHENS 1957.

VELTER,GABRIEL «Αίγινα», Επιμέλεια Κουλικούρδη Γ., ATHENS 1962.

GITAKOS, MICHAIL «Ἡ μονή Φανερωμένης ἐξ ἀπόψεως ἱστορικής, ἀρχαιολογικής και ἁγιογραφικής» ATHENS 1966.

DANTIS, XENOPHON «Αίγινα. Η αρχαία και σύγχρονη ιστορία της» ATHENS 1967.

EVANGELIDES, TRYPHON «Ιστορία του Εποικισμού της Ύδρας» ATHENS 1967.

KARAMITSOS,YIANNIS «Ύδρα νῆσος εὐτελής Δρυόπων» HYDRA 1998.

KARAMITSOS,YIANNIS «Ύδρας λεξιλόγιον το δεύτερον» HYDRA 1999.

KARGAKOS, SARANTOS «Η ναυμαχία της Σαλαμίνας· νίκη της Δημοκρατίας» PUBLICATION OF THE CULTURAL CENTRE OF PERAMA 1986.

KARYDIS, MERCURIOS «Η ιστορία της Αίγινας» ATHENS 1979.

KOULIKOURDI, Y. and ALEXIOU,SP. «Αίγινα, οδηγός για την ιστορία και τα μνημεία της» ATHENS 1954.

KOUTSIS, NIKOLAOS «Σαλαμίνος Κυνοσούρα» SALAMIS 1970.

KRIEZIS,GEORGIOS «Ἱστορία τῆς νήσου Ύδρας πρό τοῦ 1821», MARSEILLES 1988.

KONSTANTOPOULOU, CHRISTOS «Η Αίγινα στα χρόνια του Καποδίστρια» ATHENS 1968.

LIGNOS, ANTONIOS «Ἱστορία τῆς νήσου Ύδρας» Α' και Β' τόμος ATHENS 1946,1953.

MIAOULIS, ANTONIOS «Ἱστορία τῆς νήσου Ύδρας ἀπό ἀρχαιοτάτων χρόνων μέχρι τοῦ 1821» 1936.

MOUSTOPOULOS, NIKOLAOS «Η Παληαχώρα της Αιγίνης» ATHENS 1962.

MIRIKLIS, IOANNIS «Ταξίδι στην Ύδρα» ATHENS 1958.

PAPADOPOULOS, NIKOS «Η ναυμαχία της Σαλαμίνος» ATHENS 1962.

PAPANTONIOU,GEORGIOS «Ἡ ἐν Σαλαμίνι ναυμαχία» ATHENS 1950.

PAPASPYROU, A. «Η ένδοξη Ύδρα» ATHENS 1905.

PRATAKIS, ELEFTHERIOS «Η σπηλιά του Μπεκίρη των Σπετσών» ATHENS 1950.

SACHINIS, GEORGIOS «Υδραϊκή ψυχή» ΥΔΡΑ 1979

STAMATIS, KOSTAS «Αίγινα: Ιστορία - Πολιτισμός» Τόμος Β' ATHENS 1998.

STAMATIOU, GEORGIOS (editor) «Οδηγός Μουσείου Σπετσών» ATHENS 1966.

TSALLI, MINA «Σπέτσαι» ΑΘΗΝΑ 1956.

HADJIANARGYOS, ANARGYROS «Τα σπετσιώτικα» Επανέκδοση ATHENS 1979.

HADJIS, PERIKLES «Νῆσος Σαλαμίς» ATHENS 1973.